CLASSIFIED!

A TEACHERS' GUIDE TO FILM AND VIDEO
CENSORSHIP AND CLASSIFICATION

RICHARD FALCON

BRITISH FILM INSTITUTE

bfi

BFI PUBLISHING

First published in 1994 by the
British Film Institute
21 Stephen Street
London   W1P 1PL

in association with
BBFC
BRITISH BOARD OF FILM CLASSIFICATION

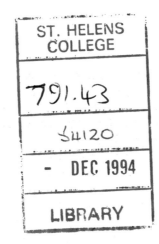
The British Film Institute exists to encourage the development of film,
television and video in the United Kingdom, and to promote knowledge,
understanding and enjoyment of the culture of the moving image. Its activities
include the National Film and Television Archive; the National Film Theatre;
the Museum of the Moving Image; the London Film Festival; the production
and distribution of film and video; funding and support for regional activities;
Library and Information Services; Stills, Posters and Designs; Research;
Publishing and Education; and the monthly *Sight and Sound* magazine.

British Library Cataloguing-in-Publication Data.
A catalogue record for this book is available from the British Library.

ISBN 0-85170-435-2

Cover design by The Senate

Printed in Great Britain by St Edmundsbury Press Ltd,
Bury St Edmunds, Suffolk

Acknowledgments

I owe much of the material in this guide to my colleagues among the part-time film and video examiners who work for the British Board of Film Classification, from whom, through papers, discussions, arguments and reports produced as part of the job of giving classification advice, I have learned and utilised a great deal. Specific acknowledgment must be made to research with young people's video usage conducted in schools during 1991-2 by Julian Wood, on which I have drawn in Part Three.

Thanks go also to the Board itself – the Presidents and the Director of the BBFC – for allowing this venture to go ahead, to the BBFC's senior management team, particularly Margaret Ford, for encouragement and support and to my overseas colleague Andrée Wright of the Office of Film and Literature Classification in Sydney and Behroze Gandhy, both of whom helped me get it off the ground.

I would like to thank Manuel Alvarado and Jim Cook for patient editorial work and for backing an occasionally controversial initiative and also to Julian Bowker for his assistance in developing the teaching materials in Part Three. Thanks also to Tricia Jenkins and Paul Mundt in providing helpful suggestions for classroom ideas.

At the BBFC, much gratitude goes to Kathy Sharp, Philippa Briggs and Natalie Brady for word processing the manuscript, Jean McMeakin for formatting it and Karen Venn for providing invaluable secretarial support when it came to clearing extract copyrights.

Alpa Patel, at the BFI, deserves special mention for the formatting, layout and typesetting. Sue Bobbermein, Natasha Murray and Mark Robertson assisted in wordprocessing and formatting.

I am grateful to the organisations and publications who gave permission for reproduction of material as illustrations, and as video clips.

Finally, I am indebted to Frances Shanahan for having put up with this for so long.

Richard Falcon, 1994

CONTENTS

**PART TWO   A BRIEF HISTORICAL ACCOUNT OF FILM AND VIDEO
                 CENSORSHIP AND CLASSIFICATION IN BRITAIN**

PART ONE
TEACHING ABOUT FILM AND VIDEO
CENSORSHIP AND CLASSIFICATION

INTRODUCTION

This study pack is intended for use in the sixth form and upper secondary school and may be of use in further education. It may be used in media studies classes or selectively in media education as part of the English National Curriculum. It is in the nature of this topic that it also provides much material for such cross curricular themes as Personal and Social Education, Citizenship and Economic and Industrial Understanding. Most of the works cited in the text are referred to by author and date; for full details see either Appendix II or III (pp. 27-30).

Censorship and the Classroom

Teaching about film and video censorship and other forms of media regulation is a difficult task for the following reasons:

- it raises issues which are unresolved, and some would say incapable of resolution, outside the classroom;
- it attempts to discuss the process with the very people it operates on: one of censorship's main rationales is to protect young people from 'unsuitable' material.

It is my hope that both these difficulties can be turned into challenges provoking constructive classroom discussion and activities in which pupils bring their own experience of the media and views of the world into play. In order to do this it is necessary to question why censorship of the media exists in all societies, albeit in different forms, and briefly face the broad pro- and anti-censorship positions from the outset so that various forms of censorship practice can be looked at productively.

Neville March Hunnings has offered a series of causal factors for the existence of film censorship which provides a good starting point:

> Censorship has an extremely complicated network of causes: psychological – many people have a compulsive need to prevent other from uttering thoughts or images which are disturbing or distasteful to them; political – governments and governing bodies have an interest in preserving stability and in preventing utterances which may upset their own policies; paternal – parents have an interest in ensuring that their children are exposed only to influences which will cause them to develop along desirable lines; social – administrators and citizens have an interest in the preservation of a healthy society and in the prevention of criminal and deviant conduct. (Hunnings, 1967, p. 383.)

A phenomenon which owes its existence to psychological, political, paternal and social causes is not one which lends itself easily to debate inside or outside the classroom, and this is why many people take refuge in assertion rather than argument when this topic is mentioned. Hunnings refers to the psychological causes of censorship as though they are confined to the realm of the aberrant mental processes of the professional moralist, but Sigmund Freud isolated the ways in which all our psyches censor their own unwelcome utterances. History is full of scapegoated groups on which the repressed messages of society's communal psyche have been projected: minority racial groups, for example. Censorship of books in the Third Reich went hand in hand with propaganda and atrocity. In Britain, however, there is the Race Relations Act, which, as an example of a product of Hunnings's social causes of censorship, attempts to prevent public utterance which could exacerbate racial injustice or cause racial violence. It is clear from these brief opening comments that some forms of censorship may appear more reasonable than others.

The political causes of censorship deserve to be looked at closely. Various forms of political censorship are evident in all societies. In the United States, which has freedom of speech, press, religion and assembly enshrined in its constitution's First Amendment of 1791, details of American casualties in the Gulf War were censored from news broadcasts in 1991, and the Hollywood 'blacklist' of the 50s, which prevented scriptwriters and directors with 'Un-American' views from working in the film industry, stand as very specific historical examples of film censorship. A consideration of political media censorship in the UK would have to take into account anti-terrorist legislation banning supporters of the IRA from speaking with their own voices on television or the controversy over BBC television's *Real Lives* documentary in 1985, which the Corporation removed from the schedules because the government objected to the appearance of interviewees who were advocating political violence. Classroom work on political media censorship could also look at patterns of ownership of the media and its effect on freedom of information and dissemination of different political viewpoints, as well as the question of whether the millions of pounds spent by the major political parties advertising their policies acts as a form of economic censorship keeping less well-funded views from the public gaze. This pack concentrates primarily, though, on the arrangements for regulation of film and video material in Britain and on their causal factors, which are largely the last two on Hunnings's list – paternal and social – as well as a factor not mentioned in this quotation: the economic. These are the areas in which film and video and most television censorship operate and it is on this ground that public disagreement occurs.

Before sketching in briefly some of these disagreements, it is necessary to note that the causal factors mentioned are not as easily separable as these comments suggest – paternal, parental and social factors are inextricably enmeshed with the political and the psychological. Guy Phelps, for example, describing the British Board of Film Censors (BBFC), as it was called in the 70s, tackles the thorny question of whether film censorship is not just a political issue, which it has always been, but whether it is a political practice:

> All censorship has political implications, and while the Board is careful to avoid explicit political interference, it is inevitable that a point of view is taken. There is little doubt that films encouraging anarchy, for example, would be banned or heavily cut on one pretext or another. Whether this is defensible in a democratic society is debatable. All that can be said is that there is only one way to banish political censorship and that is by abolishing censorship altogether. Even if that task were achieved, problems of editorial and financial control would still ensure the dominance of certain modes of expression. (Phelps, 1975, p. 271)

Paternally and socially motivated censorship is political in the sense that it necessitates the application of a particular set of values to film and video representations. Passing a film in the '15' category, which bars people under that age, is clearly not just a statement about the film, but about childhood and early adolescence. Shortening a lengthy and explicit rape scene which appears to be there merely for titillation, or removing easily copied violent techniques and glamorised weaponry from videos classified for adults as the BBFC does, are practices which are the result of value judgments about film/video and society and the relationship between them. Even the proscribing of the taboo words 'fuck' and 'cunt' for 'U'- and 'PG'-rated films is based on privileging the value systems of an audience wishing to maintain the taboo for its children over others who are not as concerned with this issue. Although political or, more properly, ideological considerations can always be read off from any classification or censorship policy or decision, it is certainly the case that no direct political censorship has taken place at the BBFC's hands since the 50s. There is a marked difference between the examples of film and video censorship mentioned above and the overtly political form of censorship which removed Peter Watkins's drama-documentary about the aftermath of a nuclear attack on Britain, *The War Game*, from British' television screens from 1965 until 1985. One reason for this is that the very existence of television changed the nature of cinema in the 60s and 70s as mass audiences turned to the new medium as the main source of entertainment and information.

The cinema audience has, since the 50s, been a predominantly young one – major Hollywood films tend to target the sixteen to twenty-five age group. Although the conventional image of the nuclear family, comprising working father, housewife mother and dependent children of school age, makes up less than 5 per cent of the population, this is the assumed norm that television addresses (Ellis, 1982, p. 115). This provides the explanation both for the 9 p.m. watershed and for the stricter censorship policies that television stations adopt for programmes transmitted at all hours. Taking the BBFC's classifications of films in 1990 as a guide, in Table 1 we can see that, according to this institution's policies of suitability, cinema is predominantly a teenage and adult medium.

It is apparent that this observation must reflect the intended audience for films, otherwise film distributors would request that their films be cut to obtain lower categories. The BBFC would only grant such requests if it felt the film in question specifically addressed younger audiences and had something to offer them. When it comes to classifying films,

Table 1
Number and percentage of films by classification

Classification	Number of films	Percentage of total
'U'	18	(4.5%)
'PG'	69	(17.4%)
'12'	50	(12.6%)
'15'	147	(37.1%)
'18'	111	(28.0%)
'R18'	0	
Rejected	1	
Total		(100%)

a large part of the work of the BBFC resides in deciding which of those films declared unsuitable for children should be given a '15' or an '18' certificate, which means that this age classification system for films largely addresses teenagers between fifteen and seventeen years old. It is for this reason that this pack concentrates on the border between '15' and '18' certification in the case studies on *Platoon* and *Madonna, Justify My Love* in Part Three.

The relevant arguments about film and video censorship, then, are those which are based not on censorship as a direct politically motivated intervention, but as a process which is grounded in paternal and social considerations. Paraphrasing arguments, while attempting to appear agnostic on them, is a tricky business and if the teacher wishes to pursue the for-and-against arguments in the classroom it is best to develop positions put by the students themselves. However, it will be necessary here to sketch in, however inadequately, two 'straw' positions which are polar in their irreconcilability.

The first may be thought of as a pure libertarian view, which holds that no institution or bureaucratic arrangement has the right to decide on the films other members of society can watch, and which does not allow that social responsibility should be on the agenda of discussions of media representations. The second is the pure moralist position, which holds that all representations should be subordinated to a notion of social responsibility, which is defined in relation to a series of moral codes by which the moralist lives and/ or believes others should be encouraged to live. There is no common ground between these positions, but there is, arguably, a symbiosis. The pure moralist position defines 'art', narrowly, as propaganda for the approved moral code, while the pure libertarian position finds value in any communication in any circumstances. Hence, on the one hand, we have a Christian pressure group defining the work of one of the most interesting and challenging of British film directors as 'filth' when it was shown late at night on Channel Four during the 80s and, on the other, we have apologists for a conscienceless 'splatter' video containing a twenty-minute gang-rape sequence avoiding the question of whether a moral dimension to representation could exist by pointing out that Shakespeare included a rape in the plot of *Titus Andronicus.*

By looking at the implications of both of these positions a little more closely, it should be possible to isolate various contentions about the subject of paternally and socially orientated media censorship for classroom discussion. This is not an attempt to elevate the 'middle ground' to a position of truth because no middle ground exists between these positions, far less an institution to represent or act upon it. The aim, instead, is to present ideas which can be mobilised in the workbook section of this pack and which will allow students to develop and refine their own ideas on the subject.

'People should be allowed to watch anything they want to watch' – the pure libertarian position

The adjective 'pure' in my designation of these debating positions indicates that both positions are essentially idealist – in the simple sense that they are rooted, not in social and economic conditions or institutional practices in the real world, but in either an ideal of personal liberty or an ideal of complete moral consensus. Without following this observation into the far reaches of philosophical enquiry, it can be productive in the classroom, particularly in work in media studies and in relation to citizenship and industrial and economic understanding, to look at why, when it comes to the consumption of media products, we are not entirely free, autonomous individuals in the way that John Stuart Mill (a favourite reference point for this position) argued that we should be. First, there is the wide gulf between the production of media products and the consumption of them.

While autonomy has been an ideal of both art cinema and independent cinema and video – from French director Alexandre Astruc's advocacy of the 'caméra stylo' which inspired the French New Wave in the 50s and 60s, to open access slots on television, it remains the case that most film and video communications are from the few to the many. The few can range from directors holding sway over a hundred million pound budget in Hollywood to a handful of independent directors who have been determined and/or fortunate enough to obtain public or other funding to make a film. Freedom of expression in film is therefore not open to everyone. There is then the question of how far those who produce and direct films aimed at a mass market are free from the constraints involved in reaching that market. Film history abounds in examples of studio interference in films such as Orson Welles's *The Magnificent Ambersons* (US, 1942).

When it comes to the distribution and exhibition of films, a further level of economic influence exerts itself. Over four thousand films are made each year worldwide and barely a tenth of these will appear on British cinema screens. When it comes to consumer freedom of choice it is also the case that a film which can afford to have a million pounds spent on an advertising campaign is going to exert more control over consumer choice than a low-budget independent film.

None of these observations provides an argument for film censorship, of course, but they do indicate why the 'pure' libertarian position I've unfairly set up is far removed from the reality of film and video production and consumption. I am free to see what other people have decided shall be commissioned, funded, produced, distributed, exhibited, promoted, transmitted, classified and censored.

Classification is also, as the information and activities in the pack serve to indicate, related to the limits already placed on the range of activities open to young people – the ability to drink alcohol legally in a pub, for example. It is in the area of adult censorship that the libertarian view that paternalism has extended beyond its acceptable social role finds much support. This falls under the 'social' cause of censorship. If it is believed that individual films have the capacity to make society less safe, the censor feels justified in cutting or rejecting them. The pure libertarian view could hold that adults should have the right to choose to expose themselves to material which may develop tastes for behaviour which is not to the benefit of society as a whole, because other activities, drinking alcohol for example, may have anti-social outcomes but are allowed by law. Or the position can claim that it is impossible for films to have such an effect at all, which moves the adherent of this view out of the cinephile camp where individuals who grieve at the historical effects of film censorship also respect the way that cinema can contribute to the very warp and weft of our consciousness.

Finally, a more practical, pure libertarian/anti-censorship position could claim that it is impossible for institutions to isolate those communications in media products which can lead to unwelcome social consequences. The meanings of films and videos can never be fixed entirely, being dependent on a range of factors, including knowledge of the world and of film, sophistication of interpretative skills, age, class, gender and other elements, and that because of this, adult censorship often boils down to one group in society imposing its values on another. This, of course, is an argument about the 'how' of censorship practice which this pack sets out to address.

'People shouldn't be allowed to see such things. It's disgusting' – the pure moralist position

The pure moralist position is uninterested in the why and how of censorship, as these questions are already answered. Sections of society who live, for example, by the strict moral codes of an organised religion, have a blueprint for life which finds investigations into, or challenges to, moral values in media representations largely superfluous. This is illustrated in the attempts of fundamentalist sections of the British Muslim community to have Salman Rushdie's novel *The Satanic Verses* banned. Or one could point to pressure groups like the National Viewers' and Listeners' Association who frequently claim that it is a matter of 'common sense' that images of sex, nudity and violence on television are detrimental to society.

If the pure libertarian view has to be balanced by the incompatibility of its notions of freedom with the workings of the market, the pure moralist's view gains much reinforcement from it. For moral campaigners, the fact that the media are in the hands of a privileged few means that media practitioners can be described as 'decadent' and 'trendy' and a public vein of support can be mined by the moralist through focusing on such pragmatic motivations as large audience figures and big box-office returns, both of which the moralist might consider achievable via an appeal to the audience's worst instincts. If the pure libertarian position has to cope with the reality of pragmatic regulation at all levels in the media, the moralist has to contend with the fact that society is no longer structured around one distinct set of moral precepts – particularly in the area of sexuality since the so-called 'sexual revolution' of the 60s which brought the moralists into the limelight as a self-styled countervailing force. The pure moralist position, then, has mostly to cope with the fact that it lays claim to a consensus which arguably does not exist.

This inevitably inadequate sketch of two 'straw' positions is intended to point up a number of problem areas which the teacher may like to introduce into classroom discussion. If the intention is to discuss the political and ethical minefield of censorship in any depth in the classroom, it is advisable to gather together material which reflects a more varied spread of opinions than the ones sketched above. What is clear is that institutions responsible for regulating media representations can adopt neither of these positions. It is the perspective of this teaching pack that there are practical, legal and economic considerations acting on how films, videos and television are regulated which can only be disentangled by looking at censorship in practice. The workbook which follows the historical account of the development of film and video classification and censorship in Britain, attempts to isolate, for classroom use, information and activities around the main areas of concern of the censor and classifier, and in particular how these relate to young audiences. One outcome of this classroom work should be an appreciation of why regulation is always with us and why the most profitable arguments are not those for and against censorship, but the ones which ask how does it work and how should it work? In this, young people as a specific media audience should feel that they are entitled to explore their own views in an informed fashion.

Censorship, Film Studies, Media Studies, and Media Education

The uses of work on censorship in film studies and media studies courses in the sixth form and further education is self-evident. This section looks at how the subject area can be employed in the upper secondary school by noting briefly how it relates to each of the key aspects of media education.

Media agencies

Because this guide focuses on the practice of classification and censorship of the media, it concentrates on the institutions which have this responsibility. The focus being also on film and video, the guide necessarily contains much information on the BBFC. This seeks to explain the 'they' in the statement 'they passed that video "15"'. It offers pupils insight into this particular media institution. I have not taken this as an opportunity for either 'censor bashing' or public relations, (although of course I am in a situation to do both of these things). I have understood 'agencies' in this context to mean not the nitty gritty of daily BBFC practice right down to when examiners drink their coffee, but the process and principles of censorship and classification operated by the organisation. Although it clearly cannot be presented to the pupils using such terms, I have defined 'agency', for the purposes of education about censorship, in terms of the meeting of various discourses – about young people and social responsibility, for example, and about those elements of social reality which the censor isolates as 'issues': images of violence and sexuality, depictions of drug use or incidence of 'bad' language, all of which are introduced as part of a case study or as individual sections in Part Three. Other real institutions are introduced and discussed in terms of this agency – e.g. television, the video and film industries, the press. Defining agency in this way also points up the common ground between censorship and education. Although many may feel that they are opposed in various ways, they share similar discourses about suitability. Although I hope, in writing this guide, that I have not summoned up the spirit of Thomas Bowdler too concretely, the difficulties of discussing censorship in the classroom will, I think, serve to reveal this common ground.

Media categories

This key aspect of media education usually examines how the forms (documentary, advertising, etc.) and genres (science fiction, soap opera, horror) and differences in the media themselves (television, radio, cinema, videos etc.) add to our understandings of texts. The 'Category System' of the BBFC offers explicit categorisation of media texts which can affect interpretation and can also interrelate with other media categories. For instance, horror films are generally rated '15' or '18' – how does this choice of category affect the viewers' expectations? Why are some genres seen as more suitable for children than others? Questions like these allow the BBFC's age-related categories to stimulate classroom activity which examines 'categorisation' in a wider sense.

Media technologies

Work on this key aspect of media education is made possible by this topic but is not central to it. The differences between videos and films tend to be defined by regulators in terms of audiences rather than their different technical features, but it is apparent that it is the specific technology of video which defines it as a medium of the home. Section 7 in Part Three of the workbook touches on this. Work on case study 2 (p. 49), which concerns itself with fictional screen violence can also raise the question of special effects, as no 'graphic' depiction of violence is possible without them unless the pro-filmic event is real (a consideration not covered in detail in this guide, which does not specifically look at television news reporting). This is an area where some pupils in the upper school often have an interest – usually in 'horror' effects – and this can be utilised without too much prompting from this guide (see press extract on p. 137). The key aspect of technologies can be touched upon in the question of whether depictions of violence – the extract from a video of *Platoon*, for example – would appear more or less 'violent' if it were to be seen on a large cinema screen in 70mm with Dolby sound.

Media languages

The accompanying video contains extracts from films and videos which connect with the classroom activities suggested in the eight study-pack sections in Part Three. The purpose here is to stimulate direct textual analysis with a distinct set of perspectives informing it, which are laid out in the relevant sections of the pack. This use of textual material in association with a discrete topic like this means that classroom activity relating directly to the texts themselves finds a clear focus which can, potentially, overcome one of the main obstacles to textual analysis in the classroom context. That is to say, there is a danger that textual analysis for its own sake can seem schematic and dry to pupils who are brought up too sharply against the difficulties of verbalising the processes by which their understanding of a text are created. Here, they have an opportunity to match their analysis against 'censor readings' of the text, and to concentrate on how these readings work with the predominant criterion of 'suitability'.

Media audiences

It is in this key area of knowledge and understanding of media education that this topic is potentially most productive in stimulating classroom activity. The classification process necessarily constructs audiences defined solely by age. Films which are not intended for children, and here one could include many European art films like *Babette's Feast* (Denmark, Gabriel Axe, 1987) or *Jean de Florette* (France/ Italy, Claude Berri, 1986), may have 'U' or 'PG' certificates which allow universal access and the category may signify nothing in itself about the film's intended audience. The mandatory categories '12', '15' and '18', though, by their definition as indications of box-office prohibitions, are the result of the construction of audiences of a certain age on the part of the classification authority. To assess whether a given text is suitable in whole or in part for a fifteen-year-old, the classifier has to construct a model of how a fifteen-year-old will respond to a given text. This process creates two audiences – one of notional fifteen-year-olds and a literal audience of classifiers who bring to the text a series of professional concerns, which automatically highlight certain aspects of it. The workbook begins with preliminary work on the literal audience constituted by the pupils themselves and each of the sections highlights work on the key aspect of audiences. The nature of the topic, as mentioned earlier, is clearly that it stimulates activity among the very group that the process of censorship and classification usually acts upon, and allows for the development of critical understanding on the part of the pupils about how such considerations as 'suitability' relate to their own viewing practices. It also allows for making explicit and validating the knowledge brought into the classroom by the pupils from outside. This, of course, indicates one or two areas of practical and pedagogical difficulty associated with the topic.

Media representations

Work on stereotyping and misrepresentation is usually given a great deal of attention in media studies courses. It is usual to propose that inequalities of power in society are also reflected in and reproduced through negative stereotyping of people, places and events in media texts. Of specific relevance in Part Three of this pack are issues relating to the representation of young people and women. However, stereotyping is one part of the much larger process of representation, in which both producers and audiences make judgments about how texts relate to 'reality'. Given that individuals and groups may have different perceptions about the reality of, say, a place or a social group, and given that interpretations of texts tend to vary, it is easy to see that representation is a complex and elusive concept.

This pack treats representation in relation to the role of the regulator. A key issue for examiners is the judgments they have to make about the level of realism in a film or video audience's likely response to this. These judgments are affected by other issues such as generic category (violence in a cartoon does not have the same kind of impact as violence in an explicit rape-revenge film), and the social norms and cultural attitudes which influence how national regulatory bodies around the world peg age levels to fix their classification ratings. But censorship and classification judgments will often turn on very detailed aspects of those visual conventions which signify a realist intent on the part of the film-maker: do we see the actual moment of impact of a blow, or is it just heard on the soundtrack? Does the camera dwell on the injuries inflicted on a victim or are these conveyed in some other way, or are they minimised? Aesthetics and ethics are very close here and judgments between interpretations such as graphic realism versus prurience and gloating can be hard to make.

The other essential contextual aspect to consider in exploring what gets represented, misrepresented or left out is the role of state and commercial institutions and agencies: the government, the Church, the legal system, lobby groups, press and television, etc. Ideological and cultural values are part of the process of production and the meaning of any film or video, and the role of agencies and their relationship to each other also needs to be examined. Any exploration of social and cultural contexts or textual meaning within media studies should include the influential role of the regulator and the process of regulation in determining what gets made, what gets shown and by whom it is seen.

Specific Difficulties with the Topic

A general problem of media education in the secondary school addressed by the BFI's *Secondary Media Education: A Curriculum Statement* (ed. Julian Bowker, 1991) is the question of how far teachers may be intruding into the private space of pupils by attempting to mobilise knowledge of the media, amassed largely outside the school walls, in the service of critical and conceptual understanding in the classroom. This is a particularly difficult problem, which is not to be underestimated, in relation to this particular topic. If the teacher is able to move beyond the effect on the pupils of peer-group pressure and bravado, which may declare that nothing is 'unsuitable' for them (and this in itself is no small problem as experience has shown) and that they have seen every possible 'unsuitable' film or video anyway, the teacher could be felt to be venturing too far into the private space of pupils by dealing with those areas of vulnerability which the classification of films and videos as a process seeks to address.

While certain media texts may be used by pupils in

their private lives as an introduction to new emotions and experiences, their responses to these texts may quite properly be something which they would prefer to keep away from the public space of the formal school curriculum. This is a particular problem in relation to representations of sex and discussions of sexuality, which is an area the teacher may have to approach with caution. Watching a sex scene in a '15' film with friends in the cinema or at home on video is a different process to considering it in the rather more public space of the classroom among mixed-gender groups, and sensitivity to the insecurity this may create will be required. This relationship between the usual consumption of media products as a private process and the production and distribution and marketing of them as a very public one is, of course, the nexus in which classification and censorship operates and, with care, problems like this can be turned to advantage.

It is probably no bad thing that the teacher's awareness of the difficulties of being *in loco parentis* while respecting the views of the class, may create the need for the teachers to become their own classifier and censor as material is chosen for this topic. The contents of this pack have also been selected bearing the problem in mind that work on the media deals often with the question of the pupils' identity and relationships with others, which as they are in the process of being formed can be fragile and prone to disruption. This relates not only to representations of sex, but to the considerations of how effective media texts are in constructing and addressing audiences of young people in ways which suggest roles and identities at a stage when the pupils may be particularly open and receptive to such strategies. Again this is central to the process by which media texts have traditionally been categorised by censors and regulators. While notions of imitation and direct emulation of media 'role models' are a reductive way of conceptualising the way young people relate to media texts, it is probably unwise to underestimate the kind of investment in screen identification figures which could well be alienating when dragged into the light of the classroom.

Work on this aspect of the topic also touches upon significant considerations in Personal and Social Education (PSE): on the contribution of media texts to self-image and self-understanding, and in the active exploration of values and the formation of attitudes.

It has been a central consideration in the writing of this teachers' guide and the production of classroom materials that the processes of paternally and socially motivated censorship and classification, whatever we may think of them in the abstract, are centrally and concretely concerned with the problems which may be created by the way the media address young people, and the way young people use the media. The value of the study of this process as part of a programme of study of the media in the classroom, is that it can contribute to one of the main goals of education generally – the production of more informed, more responsible and critically self-aware adults.

PART TWO
A BRIEF HISTORICAL ACCOUNT OF FILM AND VIDEO CENSORSHIP AND CLASSIFICATION IN BRITAIN

INTRODUCTION

This section is intended as a brief informational resource for teachers. The aim is not to set the agenda for classroom activities but to offer a basic historical/institutional framework which may be of use in stimulating comparative work relating to the classroom materials. It is important that factual information be deployed strategically as the imparting of potentially irrelevant detail sometimes militates against the engagement with ideas and the development of conceptual understanding. To be balanced against this priority is the importance of the topic of censorship and classification for classroom engagement with how extra-textual elements – social forces, media institutions, legislation – operate on the video and film texts being studied. The historical material is presented chronologically and in the knowledge that many of the secondary works referred to have long been out of print and may prove difficult to locate.

The Origins of Film Censorship in Britain

The British Board of Film Censors, as it was called until 1985, was founded by the film industry in 1912 and has, since that year, exercised responsibilities over the cinema which, by virtue of the 1909 Cinematograph Act, belong exclusively to the local authorities. The 1909 Act stipulates that cinemas should be licensed, a requirement which followed a series of well-publicised fires in music halls showing films and in the rapidly increasing number of cinemas resulting from the growth of film as a mass entertainment medium. These fires were the result initially of unsafe illuminant gases in the projection process and later by inflammable nitrate film stock. Robertson (1985), who gives, along with Hunnings (1967), the fullest account of the background to this legislation, suggests that the Act was also intended as a response to concerns expressed in that year by the Metropolitan Police to the Home Office about both fire safety and the content of the films being shown, as many of these films 'glorified crime'.

Whatever the Act's intention, it became clear in the years 1909-12 that the local authorities understood their remit to award annual licences to cinemas in wider terms than fire safety regulation, imposing as they began such conditions as: a ban on Sunday performances and on 'barking' at the door to attract customers; fixed hours of opening; and a stipulation that unaccompanied children not be allowed entry to cinemas after 9 p.m. This latter condition, rather than being the first appearance of the 'watershed' between children's and adult viewing, was more concerned with children's physical safety in public, as, unlike later media legislation, no distinction was made between films suitable for children and those suitable only for adults.

Nevertheless many of the objections of local authorities to the contents of films being shown by cinemas requiring licences were based on the notion of their suitability for children. The Watch Committee of Walsall Council objected in 1910 to film of an American boxing match because it 'tended to demoralise and brutalise the minds of young people especially' (Hunnings, 1967, p. 50) (Hunnings points out that the Johnson v. Jeffries fight was the cause of disquiet because it involved a black boxer defeating a white one), and Fulham Borough Council expressed the view that 'the character of all picture exhibitions should be carefully supervised' because the cinema was popular with children. Michael Chanan indicates that the concern that young people were being lured into crime by cinema films was a common headline in newspapers around this time and is one which attaches itself to any rapidly emerging new mass medium. (He also points out that children were often taken along to cinemas by adults for neither entertainment nor edification, but because they were better at seeing and reading the intertitles.) (Chanan, 1980, p. 255) A relatively late entry into the public controversy about the dangers of the new mass medium of cinema to children and to society in general is cited by Martin Barker (1984, p. 88) and exemplifies much of this moral disapproval of popular entertainment:

> Before these children's greedy eyes with heartless indiscrimination, horrors unimaginable are … presented night after night … terrific massacres, horrible catastrophes, motor car smashes, public hangings, lynchings. … All who care for the moral well-being and education of the child will set their faces like flint against this new form of excitement. (*The Times*, 12 April 1913.)

In such a climate of disapproval of the cinema's alleged effects on the moral education of young people, the film industry became increasingly concerned at the frequency with which magistrates were finding in favour of local authorities and against cinema exhibitors, who were appealing against the refusal of licences.

The cinema industry having organised itself into three trade associations representing the cinema hardware manufacturers (The Kinematograph Manufacturers' Association – KMA), the cinema owners (The Cinematograph Exhibitors' Association – CEA) and the distributors (The Incorporated Association of Film Renters) during the 'cinema boom' years, and fearing loss of profits if erratic local authority licensing decisions based on film content were to affect the medium's popularity, started to develop the idea of a trade censor. Overtures to this end were made to the Home Secretary in 1912, who refused to give government support as statutory responsibility lay with the local authorities.

The BBFC began its work in 1913 as a film industry body whose funding derived from submission fees charged to distributors according to the length of film submitted. The finances of the BBFC were controlled by the KMA, an arrangement deriving from the observation that this was the branch of the film industry least affected by individual censorship decisions. This 'curious arrangement' as one Home Secretary (and President of the BBFC) described it, which relies on a 'gentleman's agreement' between the trade and the BBFC for the submission of material, places the Board in a three-way relationship between the film industry, the local authorities (who retain legal responsibility for the films screened but delegate this in practice to the BBFC), and finally, the criminal law, as it was later applied to film. It is an arrangement which, in relation to film rather than video continues to this day.

Initially, after the founding of the BBFC with its first President, E. A. Redford, drawn from the Lord Chamberlain's Office of Theatre Censorship (abolished in 1968), many local authorities were unwilling to recognise the organisation and, as Guy Phelps has pointed out, 'the existence of a board of censors seemed to stimulate many councils to renewed censorial activity' (Phelps, 1975, p. 28). One such authority was Manchester City Council which continued to ban films passed by the censor and, along with a number of chief constables who were willing to express their certainty that juvenile delinquency was due to 'demoralising' effects of the cinema, urged the Home Office to appoint an official censor. This lobbying brought about the tabling of a scheme for a Home Office-appointed board, which was opposed by the trade. Such a scheme, the trade believed, would allow the local authorities to retain their full powers and thereby foster inconsistency in decision-making and would also relegate the industry to a lower place in the censorship structure.

Nevertheless, the Home Office intended to introduce official censorship in January 1917. Three events prevented this from taking place: the appointment by the industry of a new President, Liberal MP and ex-CEA chairman T. P. O'Connor, following the death of Redford; the setting up of a Cinematograph Trade Council inquiry by the National Council of Public Morals (NCPM) to look into 'the physical, social, moral and educational influence of the cinema, with special reference to young people'; and most significantly, the fall of the Asquith government, in 1916 which led to a new Home Secretary who was relatively uninterested in either the cinema or censorship.

Giving evidence to the NCPM inquiry, O'Connor offered forty-three rules which he believed would cover the field of censorship in First World War Britain. The inquiry reported back favourably on the work of the BBFC and cleared the film industry of most of the charges being laid against it in the press. In the early 20s the influential London County Council (LCC) and Middlesex County Council (MCC) passed rulings that the exclusive screening of BBFC-certificated films should be a requirement for their cinema licences, and this was followed in 1923 by a Home Office recommendation to local authorities that they adopt the LCC's and MCC's requirement, which set in place the system in operation today in which the film categories are displayed on film publicity posters and on an on-screen caption card at the start of the film.

The First Categories
From its inception, the BBFC issued two categories:

- 'U' (Universal) – which recommended the film for children's matinees; and
- 'A' (Public or later Adult) – which denoted that the film

was more suitable for adults.

These categories were advisory until the LCC's decision to adopt them in 1921 included a modification to the 'A', which stipulated that children under sixteen had to be accompanied by an adult, parent or guardian.

BBFC Policy in the Interwar Years
The latter part of the formative period for film censorship in Britain was inevitably affected by the First World War. Newsreels were exempt from the BBFC's arrangement with the trade, and during the war, O'Connor refused to deal with 'propaganda films' because in their aim of enlisting public sympathy on issues such as 'certain diseases' (i.e. venereal disease), 'illegal operations' (i.e. abortion), 'white slavery, race, suicide', etc. they were anomalous. For the BBFC in this period, film censorship reflected and contributed to the belief that film was a business aiming to profit from the production of entertainment, and any educational or artistic qualities of the cinema were denied. Robertson (1985) points out that, in practice, during the war years, a handful of pacifist films, which would be expected to contravene a number of O'Connor's rules were passed as a result of this reductionist view of the cinema's capabilities. He also indicates, as do Guy Phelps and John Trevelyan, that the existence of a pre-censorship body like the BBFC often results in films which are likely to contravene Board policy, or at least Board policy as understood by distributors, not being submitted – D. W. Griffith's *Intolerance* (US, 1916), for example, whose narrative at one point illustrates human bigotry by depicting Christ's crucifixion (contravening O'Connor's forty-third rule) or Abel Gance's *J'Accuse* (France, 1918) (rules 20 and 23).

A corollary of this disparagement of the cinema was an unfavourable view of popular cinema audiences, who were constructed by the censor as an immature mass, open to demoralisation which could undermine the institutions of family, marriage, the Church, the police, etc. John Trevelyan drew attention to the overtly acknowledged paternalism of the BBFC in the interwar years:

> Up to the last war, the Board clearly considered itself the guardian of public morality, allowing no departure from the accepted code of conduct and behaviour, the protector of the establishment, the protector of the reputation and image of Britain in other countries and the protector of cinema audiences from such dangerous themes as those involving controversial politics. (Phelps, 1975, p. 28.)

Robertson is not alone in discerning that the stricter censorship of films in relation to the theatre in this period was a result of worries caused by the fact that cinema audiences were predominantly comprised of the urban working class. As O'Connor's rules suggest, direct political censorship was clearly a part of the BBFC's practice, and although the BBFC had zealously guarded its independent status, it worked closely with the Home Office during the war and in the interwar years. In its understanding of its role as supporter of the status quo, it extended its remit from the social conventions of the day, which were understood to have unarguable moral weight (women, for example, were not to be shown drinking or 'leading immoral lives'), to political questions around Britain's relationship to the Empire and the rest of the world. This had been the case from the submission of films including scenes of riots in Johannesburg in the first year of the BBFC's existence, which were cut to meet objections by the South African government, up until after the First World War period when the Bolshevik revolution in Russia, the Spartacus uprisings in Germany and tension in industrial relations at home had created (in the British ruling classes) a fear of the possibility of revolution. This led to the banning of the early Russian films of Pudovkin and Eisenstein because they dealt with recent controversial events.

The most famous examples of political censorship of this nature includes the banning of *Dawn* (GB, Herbert Wilcox) in 1925 after pressure from the Home Office who were concerned, following representations by the German Foreign Minister, about the film's possible promotion of anti-German feeling (*Dawn* deals with the execution by the Germans of an English nurse for spying during the First World War); the refusal of a certificate to Pudovkin's *Mother* (USSR, 1926) in 1928 which, despite the campaign waged on its behalf by film-maker Ivor Montague, could only be seen via screenings by workers' film societies; and Eisenstein's *Battleship Potemkin* (USSR, 1925) which was officially rejected on grounds of violence in 1926 (see Montague, 1929).

The best example of the BBFC's worries about controversial social issues being taken up by film in the interwar years is provided by *Married Love* (GB, Alexander Butler, 1922), which has been researched and discussed at length by Annette Kuhn (1988, pp. 75-85 or *Screen*, vol. 1, no. 2, 1986, pp. 5-22). A fictional narrative co-written by birth control campaigner Marie Stopes, *Married Love*'s implicit advocacy of contraception caused a rift between the BBFC, which was in favour of banning the film because of its connections with the growing birth-control movement, and the LCC, which wanted to pass it. A compromise was reached in which the film was heavily cut, Marie Stopes's name was removed from all the publicity material for the film, and the title, which was the same as that of Marie Stopes's book on the subject (itself the subject of controversy), was changed to *Maisie's Marriages*. Kuhn's research shows convincingly how counterproductive it ultimately was even in 1922 to attempt to censor strategic filmic interventions in public debates. (Discussion of the issues around the censorship of *Married Love* would be productive in the context of PSE. Unfortunately prints of the film are unavailable.)

With the arrival of the sound film, the BBFC practice of reading scripts before production emerged as an important aspect of the organisation's remit. As Phelps (1975) has suggested, the process represented a concern to ensure that British films were not cut, but also allowed the BBFC a greater control over indigenous films than it had over American imports. For many commentators, the BBFC's guardianship of public morality led to an impoverishment of British film culture:

> To some extent the very poverty of imagination in British film production and the early contempt in which it was held, may have been due to the fact that people simply did not know what would be done and in fact was being done abroad with the film medium. (Rachael Low, 1968, p. 65.)

In the early 30s, the first wave of American horror films from Universal Studios appeared, and focused the BBFC's attention on problems arising from one particular film genre, the prime examples being *Dracula* (US, 1931) directed by Tod Browning and starring Bela Lugosi and *Frankenstein* (US, 1931) directed by James Whale and starring Boris Karloff. The former, submitted in a shorter version than the American print was passed 'A' without cuts, and the latter was passed 'A' with cuts to a sequence in which the monster throws a little girl into a lily pond to drown. Despite this cut, the LCC and MCC banned children from screenings of *Frankenstein*. This was the first occasion on which horror films had presented a problem for the BBFC. *Nosferatu: A Symphony of Horror* directed by the great German director F. W. Murnau had been banned on its submission in 1922, but no records exist to explain this decision, and most commentators believe it was due to copyright wrangles with the estate of Bram Stoker, author of *Dracula*, on which *Nosferatu* was based, rather than on its horror content.

Following the success of these two Universal horror films, the BBFC was faced with a series of now famous horror films which, like Frankenstein, attracted the interests of the Cinema Consultative Committee, a body set up by the Home Secretary in 1931 to secure greater co-operation and uniformity of standards between the local authorities and the BBFC. The BBFC warnings to local authorities, some of whom had started taking independent action about which horror films were unsuitable for children, were formalised in 1933 with the 'H' certificate. This was an advisory category suggesting that the film so designated belonged to a genre that might be thought to be unsuitable for children. Generic definition occasionally broke down as the eventual release of Abel Gance's *J'Accuse* with an 'H' in 1938 indicates. In all, thirty-one films were passed 'H' between 1933 and 1939 which, Robertson suggests, would probably have been banned were it not for this category (Robertson, 1985, pp. 51-9).

Throughout the 30s nudity and sex remained taboo areas for the BBFC, as they had been since the organisation's creation. In 1916, for example, silent star Theda Bara's first film, *A Fool There Was* (US, Frank Powell) had been refused classification because of Bara's portrayal of an amoral 'vamp' who drives men to social ruin and suicide. In the 30s the emergence of such screen 'sex goddesses' as Marlene Dietrich and Jean Harlow led to problems for the Board as films like Josef Von Sternberg's *Blonde Venus* (US, 1932) and Victor Fleming's *Red Dust* (US, 1932) were heavily cut. While Mae West was allowed to push the boundaries of sexual banter forward with *She Done Him Wrong* (US, Lowell Sherman, 1933), *Ekstase* (Czechoslovakia, Gustav Machaty, 1933) a film in which Hedy Lamarr appeared naked, was not submitted to the BBFC for fear of rejection. Bad language was also entirely unacceptable, a situation illustrated by George Bernard Shaw's clash with the BBFC over Eliza Doolittle's famous phrase 'not bloody likely' in the film version of *Pygmalion*, in 1939, which resulted in the dialogue line being passed.

The BBFC was concerned, in the 30s, to protect the image of professional people, particularly doctors, a policy reflected in the extensive cutting of King Vidor's 1938 version of A. J. Cronin's *The Citadel*, while tolerating a wave of films following the Fu Manchu series in which the Chinese were stereotyped as the 'Yellow Peril' because there was little possibility of public controversy about this issue.

The two most instructive aspects of BBFC policy in these years, however, related to Ireland, the political events in Europe leading up to the Second World War and the Hollywood gangster movies which flourished in the 30s. Many scenarios dealing with the conflict in Ireland following the civil war of 1923-4 were disapproved of by the BBFC, particularly later in the decade when an IRA bombing campaign took place in England. The popularity of Ireland as a subject of Hollywood films in the 30s is exemplified by John Ford's *The Informer* (1935) and *The Plough and the Stars* (1936), and *Parnell* (US, John M. Stahl, 1936).

The coming to power of the Nazis in Germany was accompanied by a number of films from the British and American studios (*Jew Suss* (UK, Lothar Mendes, 1934), *The House of Rothschild* (US, Alfred L. Werker, 1934), *The Wandering Jew* (UK, Maurice Elvey, 1933)), which placed the suffering of the Jews in Europe in historical context and were thus acceptable to the BBFC because they did not explicitly deal with current political realities, unlike both the anti-Russian Nazi film *Flüchtlinge* (*Refugees*, 1934), which was banned along with an anti-Nazi documentary, *Hitler's Reign of Terror* (1935). The BBFC's passing uncut of the Hollywood anti-Nazi thriller *Confessions of a Nazi Spy* (US, Anatole Litvak, 1939) was ambiguously hailed by Graham Greene as an end to the BBFC's concerns throughout much of the decade to include Nazi Germany in its brief to prevent criticism of the status quo:

> The war of nerves is on and the Censor who refused last autumn to pass a March of Time issue criticizing the Munich settlement now allows an actor made up as Dr Goebbels to refer to 'our glorious victory at Munich'. He even gives the 'U' certificate which he refuses most westerns to this picture of methodical violence and treachery. Our children must be allowed to hate and we can really feel when the British Board

of Film Censors abandons the policy of appeasement, that it really is dead at last. (Greene, 1980, p. 229.)

Worries about the effects of depictions of crime on young people had been partly responsible for the 1909 Cinematograph Act and had consistently pervaded the BBFC's policy since 1913. While scenarios involving British crime stories were discouraged, the BBFC had to contend with the Warner Bros. cycle of gangster movies, many of which had caused censorship problems in the United States. Such films as *Little Caesar* (US, Mervyn LeRoy, 1930) and *The Public Enemy* (US, William A. Wellman, 1931), according to the BBFC Annual Report of 1929, were marked by 'an atmosphere of riotous luxury' as the reward for criminal acts, and a 'continuous succession' of these films could 'invest a life of irregularity with a spurious glamour'. *The Public Enemy* was banned initially on these grounds, but by the end of the decade the BBFC felt secure enough to pass one of the genre's high points, William Wyler's *Dead End*, uncut in 1938, while still being worried enough about the similar *Angels With Dirty Faces* (US, Michael Curtiz, 1938) to demand cuts. Wyler's *Dead End* is an example of BBFC liberalism when placed in the context of the late 30s, and would make an interesting case study as a crime film/ 'problem' movie.

In 1934 Edward Short, the then President of the BBFC, responded to much criticism from the public and from The National Council for Animal Welfare for passing films in which animals, particularly horses in Westerns, had been evidently injured in the production, by calling a conference involving, among other groups, the RSPCA. The result of an advisory committee established at this conference was the Cinematograph Films (Animals) Act of 1937, which specified that no film was to be passed in which the production had involved 'the cruel infliction of pain or terror or the cruel goading of any animal to fury'. This Act is still on the statute book and the BBFC continues to remove scenes from films which contravene it.

Censorship during and after the Second World War

During the Second World War, the Ministry of Information and the Home Office approved the appointment of a Major-General to the BBFC, which at this stage had already been staffed throughout the 30s by examiners who were ex-army officers. An auxiliary censor for films which were to be shown to the services was appointed to vet films for security purposes. The most famous censorship incident of the war years concerns Winston Churchill's attempt to prevent the production of Michael Powell and Emeric Pressburger's *The Life and Death of Colonel Blimp* (UK, 1943) the story of an Anglo-German friendship between military men whose subtext concerned the necessity for Britain to forget 'gentlemanly' and old-fashioned ideas about the way war should be conducted. This was passed 'U' uncut by the BBFC in 1943.

In the immediate post war years, the development of non-inflammable 35mm film rendered the 1909 Cinematograph Act meaningless and the Wheare Committee was convened in 1947 by the government to appraise the censorship mechanics the Act had created. The Wheare Report recommended that the arrangement persist but that the category system should be revised to institute a category which would, for the first time, legally exclude children. The post war censors, President Sidney Harris and Secretary Arthur Watkins, had formulated three principles, which although they did not constitute rules – since O'Connor's time explicit rules had been eschewed by the BBFC – governed the BBFC's practice:

1. Was the story or incident or dialogue likely to impair the moral standards of the public by extenuatior crime or depreciating moral standards?
2. Was it likely to give offence to reasonably minded cinema audiences?
3. What effect would it have on children?

The Cinematograph Act of 1952 upheld the role of the BBFC and the local authorities in relation to non-inflammable film and endorsed a new category system which subsumed the advisory 'H' horror film category into the new 'X' category, which barred those under sixteen from performances. This new system followed a controversy, in 1948, over the James Hadley Chase adaptation *No Orchids for Miss Blandish* (UK, St John L. Clowes) a gangster film about the abduction of an heiress, which was passed 'A' after the original scenario had been modified at the BBFC's request and cuts had been made. The press, otherwise concerned with juvenile violence in this period, was extremely hostile to the film, and the *Monthly Film Bulletin* of April 1948 called it 'the most sickening exhibition of brutality, perversion, sex and sadism ever to be shown on the cinema screen'. The press reaction and the public outcry it attempted to mobilise caused Harris to apologise to the Home Office for his misjudgment. It hardly needs stating that *No Orchids* looks pretty innocuous when viewed today.

The decisions of the BBFC were necessarily dictated by its assessment of social trends, which in practice relies on a sensitivity to current controversies and concerns articulated and exploited by the press. This is nowhere clearer than during the 50s, the years of the appearance of the 'teenager' as a market force in affluent postwar Britain, and the consequent anxieties among opinion-formers about the effect of the mass culture targeted at these young consumers. Although Harris and Watkins's three principles allowed for a much more liberal approach to film censorship than the pre-war BBFC had conducted, the question of 'depreciating moral standards' was prominent in the press in the 50s and almost exclusively linked to the 'problem' of teenagers. The near hysteria of the press about Teddy boys and other working-class youth subcultures emerging from the 'consumer society' meant that it must have been difficult for the BBFC to include teenagers, increasingly emerging also as the main consumers of films, as part of its construction of the 'reasonably minded cinema audience'.

During the 50s, with the arrival of television, cinema

audiences began to decline, a situation which Hollywood attempted to combat by such means as the introduction of CinemaScope and a targeting of the youth audiences via, among other measures, the production of 'teen movies', which included the science fiction 'creature features', aimed at drive-ins and double bills and 'rock movies'. It was the latter genre which focused the press's insistence on a largely fictional 'teenage crime wave' in the cinema, particularly when, in 1956, the release of Bill Haley's rock 'n' roll film *Rock Around the Clock* (US, Fred F. Sears), which was passed 'U' with no cuts by the Board, was accompanied by what were described as 'cinema riots'. *The Wild One* (US, 1953), directed by Laslo Benedek, brought the BBFC up against this. The question of the teenage audience and juvenile crime and its history in relation to the Board is the subject of case study 1 in Part Three of this guide.

Initially, the 'X' certificate was avoided by the major distributors in the 50s, who believed that the cinema-going habit would decline with a consequent loss of profits if too many films excluded the under-sixteens. 'X' films became associated in the public mind with European films like Ingmar Bergman's *Smiles of a Summer Night* (Sweden, 1955) whose subtitles were often amended in the diction of euphemism (in *Smiles*, for example, 'lust' was changed to 'passion' and 'lecherous fantasies' to 'unspeakable dreams'), and which were screened at small independent cinemas. Because the category very soon became associated with sex in the public mind, the Hammer studios, who with their production of science fiction and horror films in the 50s had eschewed the family audience, were able to deploy it as a positive marketing device. It was used in the title, for example, of their successful television spin-off *The Quatermass Experiment* and *X The Unknown*, and the Hammer films of the 60s and early 70s, whose sexual and horror contents were partly dictated by the studio's negotiations with the BBFC on standards in these areas, were often heralded in posters as 'another "X" film from the Hammer studios'. In this way the 'X' certificate became a marketing tool in the hands of independent British companies like Hammer, Woodfall and Bryanston, whose importance to the film industry grew as it reorganised itself internally to respond to falling audiences and the need for product which would distinguish itself from television.

John Trevelyan became Secretary of the BBFC in 1958 after having worked for eight years as an examiner, two under his predecessor John Nicholls, who was forced to resign following criticisms of his performance by the industry. Trevelyan was eager, in the face of the emphatic social changes that were taking place in the late 50s, as well as the cinema's changed status as less of a mass medium than television, to distance the BBFC from the overt paternalism of the Board under previous secretaries. In 1960, he stated that:

> The BBFC cannot assume responsibility for the guardianship of public morality. It cannot refuse for exhibition adult films that show behaviour which contravenes the accepted moral code, and it does not demand that 'the wicked' should always be punished. It cannot legitimately refuse to pass films which criticise 'the Establishment' and films which express minority opinions. (John Trevelyan, 'The Censor's Reply', *Encounter*, September 1969, p. 63.)

Despite the liberalism of Trevelyan's public pronouncements, his achievement was to follow as closely as possible behind public trends rather than race ahead of them, and it is an irony that, whereas liberal decisions such as *Dead End* in the context of the late 30s could take place within a fairly secretive BBFC given to occasionally illiberal statements of policy, the reverse was often the case during Trevelyan's well-publicised tenure.

The clearest signs of the social change within which the Board was operating in the 60s was the wave of British social realist films taking their cue from the independent Free Cinema films and the kitchen sink school of 50s British political drama, following on from the unexpected success, despite its 'X' certificate, of *Room at the Top* (UK, Jack Clayton, 1959). The 'X' certificate was earned according to the *Sunday Express*'s critic on 25 January 1957, 'not for meretricious horror or peephole sex, but for sheer, blatant honesty … in this case at least, and at last, the 'X' certificate looks like a badge of honour'. Most of these working-class dramas, including *Look Back in Anger* (UK, Tony Richardson, 1959), *Saturday Night and Sunday Morning* (UK, Karel Reisz, 1960) and *A Kind of Loving* (UK, John Schlesinger, 1962), all wore the same badge. It would have been impossible for a censor at this time to uphold the traditional BBFC view that films were mere entertainment from which social comment should be excluded, any more than it would have been possible to miss the social implications of the Obscene Publications Act (OPA) of 1959. This law, although it specifically excluded films intended for public exhibition, occasioned a series of celebrated test cases in relation to literature: the much publicised *Lady Chatterley's Lover* trial of 1960, which resulted in D.H. Lawrence's 1928 novel being freely available for the first time since its initial publication, and the subsequent cases against John Cleland's eighteen-century erotic picaresque novel *Fanny Hill, Memoires of a Woman of Pleasure* in 1963 and Hubert Selby's *Last Exit to Brooklyn*, which led to the implicit de-censorship of literature (magazines and journals continued to be prosecuted).

This process of de-censorship during the 60s, which, a close look at the above cases would reveal to be by no means a smooth or inevitable one, culminated in the 1968 Theatres Act, which not only abolished the prior censorship of plays but prevented private prosecutions of plays under the OPA (although Mary Whitehouse circumvented this in 1980 by prosecuting Michael Bogdanov under the Sexual Offences Act of 1956 for having allegedly, with Howard Brenton's play *The Romans in Britain,* 'procured an act of gross indecency between two actors'). The OPA, with its reference to the work as a whole and its stipulation that it is the 'tendency to deprave and corrupt' persons likely to see or hear or read the material which has to be established in law, opened the way to the expert witnesses and the consideration of individual and wider contexts for such material.

In the early 60s, members-only cinema clubs started to appear which were able to circumvent the 1909 Cinematograph Act's licensing requirement by charging membership fees to an exclusively adult clientele. The first of these was The Berkeley in Tottenham Court Road which was opened in 1960 by Kenneth Rive with a screening of the still banned *The Wild One,* with Trevelyan officiating at the opening ceremony. Very soon it became clear that many of these clubs were destined to become sex film clubs, thus creating a ghetto for film material away from the mass audience which was still at the heart of the BBFC's understanding of its duties.

With the steady increase in the 60s of the number of films being placed in the 'X' category by the BBFC (219 in 1969, more than the combined number of 'U' and 'A' films, compared with twenty-eight in 1956), the Board proposed a revision of the category system which would bring it closer to Trevelyan's idea of a 'graded introduction to the adult world' (Trevelyan, 1973, p. 81). The suggestion was to introduce a new category 'AA', denoting that the film was suitable for exhibition to people of fourteen or over, making the 'A' advisory ('parents/guardians are advised that the film contains material they might prefer children under fourteen years not to see') and raising the age of admission to 'X' category films from sixteen to eighteen years.

When John Trevelyan retired in 1971, he had presided over twelve years of film history during which the cinema and British society had changed enormously. Despite the continuing practice of adult censorship, against which Trevelyan himself polemicised after retirement, the cinema had moved away from family audiences and towards a fragmented audience of mostly young adults during the 60s, a situation which, along with the socio-cultural upheavals of the years, had led to the questioning of many areas of morality about which the Board was traditionally concerned.

In the early 70s, pressure groups such as The Festival of Light (FOL) and Mary Whitehouse's National Viewers' and Listeners' Association (NVLA), which had grown out of the Women of Britain Clean Up TV Campaign, were spurred on in their campaigns against the so-called 'permissive society' by the report of an unofficial committee to investigate pornography set up by the Labour peer Lord Longford. The Longford Report's recommendations that the 'public good' test of the 1959 OPA should be replaced by a test of 'outraging contemporary standards of decency or humanity' were clearly influenced by Longford's personal beliefs as a Christian who saw pornography as a threat to 'church, state and family'. Despite the media circus surrounding the publication of the report, its lack of academic rigour was apparent along with its not-so-hidden agenda, and its influence was slight. Nevertheless, NVLA's campaigning against allegedly indecent plays on BBC television had won it some influence over the broadcasting institutions, and as the most visible display of 'permissiveness' was undoubtedly the cinema, this too became the object of NVLA's scrutiny.

Trevelyan's successor Stephen Murphy was not only placed in the firing line of these pressure groups intent on orchestrating a 'backlash' against the dominant social mood of the 60s, but was also faced with a number of difficult films: Ken Russell's *The Devils* (UK, 1971) (which caused controversy with its mixture of sex and religion and which had been cut by Trevelyan for 'X' but not released until Murphy was in the censor's chair), Stanley Kubrick's *A Clockwork Orange* (UK, 1971) and Sam Peckinpah's *Straw Dogs* (UK, 1971) (the latter never having been passed on video by the BBFC). All of these films retain their notoriety today and the reception of each illustrates clearly the vulnerability of the censor to the power of the press as well as the marketability for the industry of controversy (Barr, 'Straw Dogs, A Clockwork Orange and the Critics', *Screen*, vol. 13, no. 3, 1972, pp. 17-31). The BBFC passed *Straw Dogs* 'X' with cuts to two scenes in 1972, when it opened in London to a barrage of negative criticism from newspaper reviewers, thirteen of whom signed a letter to *The Times* on 17 December 1972 in which they questioned the BBFC's decision and described the film as 'excessive in its effect and likely to contribute to the concern expressed from time to time by many critics over films which exploit the very violence they make a show of condemning'. *A Clockwork Orange*, in contrast, received positive reviews, but was constructed as a 'problem' film by a series of lurid reports concerning alleged copycat crimes. Stanley Kubrick, possibly in response the British press's persistent attacks on the film withdrew all prints of it from circulation in Britain, where, following its highly successful first run, it has not been shown legally since.

Stephen Murphy's embattled stewardship of the BBFC ended with his resignation in 1975, when he was succeeded by James Ferman. In the year of Ferman's arrival at the BBFC, the implications of films being left vulnerable to prosecution at common law were made clear by a case against two sex education films from Sweden, *Language of Love* and *More About the Language of Love* (Phelps, 1975, pp. 72-3). In the case of *Language of Love*, the President and Secretary of the BBFC were charged with aiding and abetting an indecent exhibition. The case against them was dismissed and the film found not to be indecent by an Old Bailey jury but *More About the Language of Love*, which had been rejected by the Board but passed by the GLC, was successfully prosecuted. It was clear that the test of indecency, defined by one judge as 'anything which an ordinary man or woman would find to be shocking, disgusting or revolting', referred to standards of propriety or manners which are a problematic basis for judging the acceptability of works of art. Acting in evidence given by the BBFC, the Law Commission recommended in a 1976 report that cinema films should be brought under the OPA, which allowed for defences under the public good, required that the work be proven 'corrupting and depraving', which meant that a notion of immorality become the test rather than an affront to manners. As the BBFC preferred to judge films from this perspective – it had in any case begun to draw a distinction between 'manners' dealt with by categorisation, and 'morals' – it was able to persuade the Home Office in its drafting of the Criminal Law Act 1977 to bring films within the OPA and remove the risk of private prosecution for obscenity of works already judged by the BBFC. A provision was included which stipulated that no proceedings could be instituted except with the consent of the Director of Public Prosecutions (DPP).

Where, previously, 'indecency' had been largely a matter of the explicitness of screen representations, usually of sex, the obscenity test required that film sequences be assessed in context for their possibly corrupting influence, which was being understood more and more in terms of the placing of viewers in a sadistic relationship to screen victims of violence and, more often than not, the screen victims of sexual violence.

In 1982, Ferman (Ferman, 'Censorship Today', *Films Illustrated,* vol. 9, no. 98, October 1979, pp. 62-7) drew attention to the fact that in 1976 the Board had viewed fifty-eight films in which there were scenes of 'explicit rape' (a remarkable statistic given that the Board views, on average, four hundred or so films a year). It was the glorification of crimes of violence like rape which the Board began to consider 'obscene', rather than the level of explicitness of sex scenes. Pornography involving children was highlighted as a problem in the late 70s and to attempt to control its import into this country, the 1978 Protection of Children Act (PCA) included a new test of legality for films in Britain. Because it was unlikely that juries would not find child pornography obscene under the OPA and also unlikely that child pornographers would submit their work to the BBFC for classification, the PCA was also intended to protect child performers from being exploited by film-makers. The PCA makes it illegal not only to take indecent photographs of children but to publish, or distribute, them or possess them with this intention. The emphasis on still pictures and indecency means that context is no mitigation and that the

child has to appear in the shot which is judged to be indecent. Mainstream films which have fallen foul of this Act in the Board's view include Louis Malle's *Pretty Baby* (US, 1978), Martin Scorsese's *Taxi Driver* (US, 1976) and, because its purpose is to prevent exploitation of performers from abuse by prohibiting the visual result of the abuse, the Act is closer in spirit to the Cinematograph Films (Animals) Act of 1937 than it is to the OPA.

During this period of legal reform in connection with the regulation of cinema films, the Callaghan government in 1977 set up a Home Office Committee on Obscenity, Indecency, Violence and Film Censorship, chaired by philosophy professor Bernard Williams. When the Committee published its conclusions in 1979, it included a recommendation that sexual depictions should no longer be subject to the criminal law if their performers were neither under age, nor made to suffer actual physical harm. Although the Committee also recommended the repeal of the OPA, it concluded that violent and sadistic sexual depictions on film constituted such a major social problem that film censorship even for adults should continue. The Act has not been repealed but Ferman has since observed, and it is currently part of BBFC thinking, that the type of work which the Committee thought should be censored for adults, namely those which had 'no purpose or justification other than to reinforce or sell the idea that it can be highly pleasurable to inflict injury, pain or humiliation (often in a sexual context) on others', (Williams para. 12.10) is exactly the type covered by the OPA's notion of the work which may have a tendency to deprave and corrupt'.

The Current Category System and Video Censorship
When the Williams Committee discussed the categories 'U', 'A', 'AA' and 'X' which had been in use since 1970, it observed that the numerical age categories used throughout the rest of Europe were more communicative and less liable to misinterpretation. 'AA' for example, which was considered to denote 'adult accompaniment' meant instead that no person

under fourteen would be admitted, and the 'X' was assumed by many people to denote sex films.

The change from 'X' to '18' would remove much of this connotation. For the 'AA' category, Williams suggested raising the minimum age from fourteen to sixteen, since fourteen, falling right in the middle of puberty for many children, could be an age when more adult material might add confusion to a possibly already confusing stage. Williams recommended sixteen, the official school-leaving age and the age of sexual consent, but both the film industry and local authorities opposed this on the grounds that sixteen was too close to eighteen for easy discrimination. Fifteen, which would be at least post-puberty for most children, was proposed by the BBFC and accepted. The advisory category 'A' was changed to 'PG' which, like the American rating, spells out its meaning as 'parental guidance' and is accompanied by the explanation that 'some scenes may be unsuitable for young children'. The 'U' category remained the same.

In 1982, Parliament decided to follow the recommendation of the Williams Committee and close the loophole which had permitted bogus cinema clubs to evade both censorship and fire and safety regulations by offering 'instant membership' at the door. The 1982 Cinematograph (Amendment) Act required the licensing of all cinemas operated for private gain, which meant that all films shown in commercial clubs would be subject to scrutiny. For these premises, a new film category, the 'R18' was introduced, to be used for films containing more explicit sexual depictions that would be acceptable in the public adult category. Non-profit-making film societies, or non-commercial premises like the National Film Theatre, are exempt and can still show uncensored films. The three Cinematograph Acts have now been consolidated in the Cinema Act 1985.

In the early 80s with the development of the video recorder as an affordable piece of domestic consumer technology, much attention was drawn to the new mode of consumption of feature films. By 1982, one in ten British households was equipped with a video recorder and there were more video shops in Britain than bookshops. The sheer visibility of video as a medium in the high street and its rapid penetration as a leisure form meant that it was inevitably a subject which began to fill the popular press, and as early as 1 September 1982, the *Sun* had as its headline, 'Fury Over Video Nasties'. The phrase 'video nasties' was employed far more often than it was defined, but the *Sun* referred to a number of videos which had been subject to a successful destruction order following a prosecution by the DPP under the OPA.

By the summer of 1983, thirty-two titles had been entered on the DPP's list, comprising video films that had either been found obscene under the OPA or were either currently the subject of legal proceedings or were being considered for prosecution by the DPP. These were for the most part videos of films which had never been submitted to the BBFC, more often than not imported horror films from the United States or Italy, or films which had been cut by the BBFC for their cinema release and had been transferred onto video in uncut form among the vast amount of material which was being made available for rental or sale. Although worries about the possibility of unrestricted access to extreme material on video, which were expressed with varying degrees of genuine concern as well as with hyperbole and excess in some quarters, were very similar to those expressed during the development of film as a mass medium in the early years of the century. The situation differed in at least one crucial respect. Whereas the cinema was a medium developing new forms and experimenting with new material, video was, in the early 80s, a new transmission system for material which already existed on film and for which, as we have seen, diverse and fragmented audiences had grown. The DPP's list of prosecutable videos was therefore not the sole cause of concern for those who considered video a problem, as a great deal of material passed 'X' (later '15' and '18') by the BBFC in the 70s was unfamiliar to the large family audiences coming to video from television, which is watched 'by the family as a whole' and is consequently monitored according to the strictest standards of any audiovisual medium (see *Hunt Report On Broadcasting* ITAP-Information Technology Advisory Panel, 1982, HMSO and Ellis, 1982, p. 115). The appearance in the home of unfamiliar material along with some material in 1981-2 which would not have been allowed on the cinema circuits, created a situation in which concern could border on, and often spill over into, moral panic.

Aware that underlying the sensationalist headlines in the popular press was a genuine problem relating to insufficient consumer safeguards, the video industry's trade association, the British Videogram Association (BVA), which had been set up to represent the interests of British producers and distributors of pre-recorded videocassettes and videodiscs, particularly in relation to copyright, approached the BBFC to investigate the means by which pre-recorded video might become subject to the same system of certification which had operated in Britain for theatrical films. The BBFC suggested setting up a working party and its report, published in January 1983, recommended that a voluntary code of practice be developed along these lines, using the recently transformed categories and adding two new categories. These were (1) 'Uc' which provided the additional information to the video retailer that this video is 'particularly suitable for children', indicating that the shopkeeper may wish to stock a title with this category in a special children's section; and (2) the 'R18' or 'Restricted 18', which, by analogy with its use for cinema as a category which restricts films to specially segregated licensed cinemas (such as clubs), defines such tapes as 'sex articles' and restricts them to licensed sex shops. This system of self-regulation had been referred to by government speakers in the House of Commons in the scores of questions which were put relating to the press controversy about unregulated video.

The Conservative election manifesto for the June 1983 election, however, placed emphasis on introducing legislation to halt the 'dangerous aspect of violent and obscene video-cassettes'. After the election the Video Recordings Bill was introduced by private members' ballot. Instead of following the pattern of a piece of legislation aimed at curbing violence in children's comics, the Children and Young Persons (Harmful Publications) Act 1955, which was also drafted in a climate of considerable press comment and consequent public concern and made comics subject to the criminal law, the Video Recordings Bill aimed to make provision for a system of pre-censorship for all video works, a system which would have statutory support. The aims of the Bill were thus necessarily controversial, promising as it did to raise the spectre of formal government involvement in the prior censorship of audiovisual forms, a spectre which had been at rest since the Home Office's attempt to introduce official film censorship in 1917. A firmer academic foundation than the impressionistic and exaggerated press treatment of the problem of unregulated video works and the presumed ease of access for children to unsuitable material was needed to underpin the passage of the Bill through Parliament, and The Parliamentary Group Video Enquiry which established itself during 1983 claimed to provide this. 'An informal group of Parliamentarians and churchmen', as it described itself, the group published an interim report in November 1983, the sociological survey into the degree of access children had to unsuitable videotapes having been rushed through in time for it to be used in the Commons committee stage of the Bill (see Barlow and Hill (eds.), 1985 and Barker (ed.) 1984).

This interim report claimed that 40.4 per cent of school children aged six and upward had seen at least one of the videos on the DPP's list, and this finding made headlines immediately. From *The Times* to the *Sun,* the notion that '(nearly) 1 in 2 children have seen video nasties' was widespread. The speed with which its research was produced and the direct reliance on the respondents' answers to its questionnaire without consideration of the variables which always make such conclusions at best doubtful (peer-group pressure to claim experiences that the child had not had, inadequate recognition of listed film titles, misunderstanding of the questionnaire's purpose, etc.) have meant that the report has since been viewed with extreme scepticism in academic circles, but it served to fuel further the 'video nasties controversy' which expedited the Video Recordings Bill through Parliament.

The Video Recordings Act (VRA) was placed on the statute book in 1984 and made it an offence for a video recording to be sold or hired, offered to a customer or stocked if it contains a work which has not received a classification certificate from the body designated under the Act to confer it. In July 1985, the President and Vice Presidents of the BBFC were designated as the authority charged with making arrangements for classification of video works on the understanding that this work would be carried out by the BBFC. This meant that a traditionally small organisation had greatly to expand – in 1975, James Ferman's first year as Secretary of the BBFC, it had only four examiners out of a small staff of eleven; in 1986 it had a staff of fifty – in order to take on the classification of a vast backlog of video works. In 1986, for example, the BBFC viewed 348 cinema films under the Cinemas Act 1985 and classified 4,464 videos under the VRA.

Apart from the greatly increased number of submissions and consequent increase in the size of the BBFC, the Board's work changed in the latter half of the 80s in a number of ways. The VRA introduced a special test for video – that of suitability for viewing in the home – which necessitates differential standards between the same material on video or film, particularly in relation to extreme violence. A further significant development in the BBFC's treatment of video is the submission of a large number of untranslated videos from Commonwealth countries: a significant proportion of the examining staff of the BBFC are recruited from ethnic minorities, and bring cultural knowledge to bear on the process of classification as well as fluency in the languages of the submitted material, namely Hindi, Punjabi, Urdu, Gujarati, Cantonese, Mandarin, Arabic, Greek and Turkish. Before its designation under the VRA, the BBFC had

been required to make arrangements for the hearing of appeals from any video distributor who wished to challenge an individual category decision. The Video Appeals Committee was set up and chosen in consultation with the Home Office and comprises ten persons, some selected for their legal experience, all because of their standing in public life and their independence of the Home Office, the video industry and the BBFC. There have been very few appeals to the Committee, the most famous occurring in 1990 when the distributors of an Urdu language video, *International Guerillas* (Pakistan, 1988) appealed against the BBFC's refusal to grant a certificate because it could be seen to contravene the laws relating to criminal libel, in this case against a named individual, Salman Rushdie, who was depicted as the film's villain. This appeal was upheld following the submission to the Committee of an anti-censorship statement by Salman Rushdie himself. A second body, the Video Consultative Council (VCC) was set up in order to satisfy the need for the BBFC to be accountable, not only to the Home Office to which, since 1985, it has submitted an Annual Report on the organisation's activities, but also to the views of the video public. The broadly based VCC comprises representations of the local authority associations for England, Scotland, Wales and Northern Ireland, representatives of the video industry and individuals with a wide range of experience and expertise. The job of the VCC is to monitor the BBFC's standards at quarterly meetings.

In 1989, the BBFC, introduced a new '12' category, which barred admission to any child still in primary school, but which made suitable films available to the full range of teenagers, particularly that watershed age, the first year of secondary school. *Batman* (US, Tim Burton 1989), that year's Hollywood blockbuster, was the first film to carry this new category. The BBFC also administers on a voluntary basis the Video Packaging Review Committee (VPRC), whose logo appears on approved video sleeves. This voluntary system has since 1987 sought to prevent undue offence being caused to members of the public by explicitly violent or sexual imagery on the covers of videocassettes. The need for such a body had been noted as early as 1983 in the report back of the BVA's working party, which indicated the major role played by offensive packaging in the public's image of the video industry and in its susceptibility to the press exaggeration about 'video nasties'. A similar review procedure for trade advertising and posters was set up under the Video Advertising Review Committee (VARC). The two video trade papers (*Video Trade Weekly, Video Business*) attend as members of the VARC and refuse to carry any advertising in their own publications which has not been given prior approval by the Committee.

The BBFC has no influence over the feature films shown on the terrestrial networks, although schedulers often use BBFC certificates as a guide for the suitability of films for certain time slots. Standards in television are monitored by the Broadcasting Standards Council, which was established in 1988 by the Home Secretary to 'consider the portrayal of violence, of sex, and matters of taste and decency in broadcast and video works'. The BSC's job is to draw up codes to convey these areas, to monitor television programmes, receive and act on complaints in such areas and publicise their findings, and to undertake research in these areas. At the end of 1988, the BBFC was approached by Sky Television (later BSkyB) with a view to classifying all the films they would be showing on their satellite movie channel. Differential standards have thus been developed by each of the media to children and to the vulnerable of all ages.

As with the early days of cinema, the problem facing censors and classifiers across all of these media is to balance the need to protect children and the vulnerable while preserving the freedoms and choices that the new media have introduced. The BBFC's Annual Report for the year it first considered satellite standards lays out the basis for differential standards.

Film classification continues to set the standard because it is normally the first medium of publication and the one attracting the greatest attention from the press. But film itself occupies a smaller and smaller proportion of the Board's time. That may change, of course, since cinema in Britain entered a new expansionist phase in 1988, with more admissions than for many years and more new cinemas being built than at any time since the Second World War. Nevertheless, far more people in Britain and in other parts of the world, now see films principally on video, or through the ever-widening gamut of televisual media. As the Board's professional attention turns to these other modes of distribution, a range of standards will begin to develop based on the accessibility of the particular medium to children and the degree of private and deliberate choice for adults (Ferman, BBFC Annual Report 1988, June 1989).

APPENDIX I   Extracts from Legislation Relating to Censorship

Video Recordings Act 1984

4(1)   The Secretary of State may by notice under this section designate any person as the authority responsible for making arrangements:

(a) for determining for the purposes of this Act whether or not video works are suitable for classification certificates to be issued in respect of them, having special regard to the likelihood of video works in respect of which such certificates have been issued being viewed in the home;

(b) in the case of works which are determined in accordance with the arrangements to be so suitable:

    (i)   for making such other determinations as are required for the issue of classification certificates, and
    (ii) for issuing such certificates, and

(c) for maintaining a record of such determinations (whether determinations made in pursuance of arrangements made by that person or by any person previously designated under this section), including video recordings of the video works to which the determinations relate.

Protection of Children Act 1978

1(1)   It is an offence for a person:

(a) to take, or permit to be taken, any indecent photograph of a child (meaning in this Act a person under the age of 16); or

(b) to distribute or show such indecent photographs; or

(c) to have in his possession such indecent photographs with a view to their being distributed or shown by himself or others; or

(d) to publish or cause to be published any advertisement likely to be understood as conveying that the advertiser distributes or shows such indecent photographs, or intends to do so.

(2)   For purposes of this Act, a person is to be regarded as distributing an indecent photograph if he parts with possession of it to, or exposes or offers it for acquisition by, another person.

(3)   Proceedings for an offence under this Act shall not be instituted except by or with consent of the Director of Public Prosecutions.

Cinematograph Films (Animals) Act 1937

1(1)   No person shall exhibit to the public, or supply to any person for public exhibition (whether by him or by another person), any cinematograph film (whether produced in Great Britain or elsewhere) if in connection with the production of the film any scene represented in the film was organised or directed in such a way as to involve the cruel infliction of pain or terror on any animal or the cruel goading of any animal to fury.

(2)	In any proceedings brought under this Act in respect of any film the court may (without prejudice to any other mode of proof) infer from the film as exhibited to the public or supplied for public exhibition, as the case may be, that a scene represented in the film as exhibited or supplied was organised or directed in such a way as to involve the cruel infliction of pain or terror on an animal or the cruel goading of an animal to fury, but (whether the court draws an inference or not) it shall be a defence for the defendant to prove that he believed, and had reasonable cause to believe, that no scene so represented was so organised or directed.

The Obscene Publications Act 1959 & 1964

27	Under section 1 of the Obscene Publications Act 1959, an article is deemed to be obscene 'if its effect or (where the article comprises two or more distinct items) the effect of any one of them is, if taken as a whole, such as to tend to deprave and corrupt persons who are likely, having regard to all relevant circumstances, to read, see or hear the matter contained or embodied in it'.

## APPENDIX II	Research Referred to in the Guide

Barlow, Geoffrey and Alison Hill, *Video Violence and Children,* London, Hodder & Stoughton, 1985.
A mixture of pro-censorship, campaign rhetoric and the empirical research results of surveys carried out by the 'Parliamentary Group Video Enquiry' in 1983 into children's video viewing. It also contains the results of further surveys by the NSPCC into children and video, and a survey of paediatricians' experiences. The research was used to bolster argument for the passing of the Video Recordings Act in 1984.

Docherty, David, *Violence in Television Fiction, Public Opinion and Broadcasting Standards,* 1st Annual Review 1990, London, John Libbey, 1990.
A survey of public attitudes towards the portrayal of violence in television fiction sponsored by the Broadcasting Standards Council.

Gunter, Barrie, *Dimensions of Television Violence,* London, Gower, 1985.
Mixes an audience survey with psychologically-based research involving panels of test viewers watching extracts of violent depictions from television. It also contains a survey of television viewing patterns.

Hargrave, Andrea Millwood, (ed.), *A Matter of Manners? The Limits of Broadcast Language,* BSC Research Monograph 2, London, John Libbey, 1991.
The results of a survey of viewers' attitudes to swearing in life and on television, and essays by media practitioners on their experiences of the subject.

Levy, Mark R., (ed.), *The VCR Age, Home Video and Mass Communication,* California, Sage Publications, 1989.
Papers by different researchers into video usage and contains two articles on adolescent video use in Sweden and the United States.

Malamuth, Neil and Edward Donnerstein, *Pornography and Sexual Aggression,* California, Academic Press, 1984.
Psychologically based empirical research which concludes that depictions of violence towards women in pornography and other media products can promote aggressive attitudes to women in real life in predisposed men.

The following two books contain useful research findings on video as a medium:

Alvarado, Manuel, (ed.), *Video World-Wide, An International Study,* London Unesco/John Libbey, 1988; and **Levy, Mark R.**, (ed.), *The VCR Age. Home Video and Mass Communication,* California, Sage Publications, 1989.
The former looks at the social aspect of video technology in twenty five countries, the latter collects together papers by different researchers into video usage and contains two articles on adolescent video use in Sweden and the United States.

APPENDIX III   Suggestions for Further Reading

This is by no means an exhaustive reference list on censorship. The entries have been selected for their direct bearing on film and video.

A   Source material

Barker, Martin (ed.), *The Video Nasties: Freedom and Censorship in the Media,* London, Pluto Press, 1984.
A collection of seven articles written as a response to the newspaper campaigns against so-called 'video nasties' in the early 80s and the methodology and findings of the Parliamentary Group Video Enquiry. This contains useful comparative material for use with Barlow and Hill (1985).

Hunnings, Neville March, *Film Censors and the Law,* London, George Allen & Unwin Ltd, 1967.
An extremely thorough historical study in comparative law concerning film censorship in Britain, the United States, Canada, Australia, Denmark, France and Soviet Russia. Contains many observations on censorship of continuing value and relevance.

Kuhn, Annette, *Cinema, Censorship and Sexuality 1909-1925,* London, Routledge, 1988.
Kuhn uses three case studies of films to investigate the role of pressure groups in shaping discourses about sexuality in the cinema during the early years of the BBFC. Contains a thorough chapter on the beginnings of film censorship in Britain.

Montagu, Ivor, *The Political Censorship of Films,* London, Gollancz, 1929.
Montagu gives an account of the difficulties the Film Society Movement had in the 20s importing and screening Russian films like Vsevolod Pudovkin's *Mother* and Sergei Eisenstein's *Battleship Potemkin.*

Phelps, Guy, *Film Censorship,* London, Gollancz, 1975.
Phelps takes the controversy over a number a films in the early 70s as a starting point for a discussion of the network of influences, political, social and economic at work in the practice of film censorship and gives a detailed account of the years of Stephen Murphy as BBFC Secretary.

Phillips, Baxter, *Cut: The Unseen Cinema,* London, Lorrimar, 1975.
A short, heavily illustrated and highly individual survey of the international history of film censorship focusing mostly on the American experience.

Robertson, James C., *The British Board of Film Censors. Film Censorship in Britain 1896-1950,* London, Croom Helm, 1985.
Robertson attempts a systematic social history of film censorship in Britain. It offers an extremely useful breakdown of film themes and genres in the 30s and sets the BBFC's work in the context of the American ratings system, pointing out what he sees as a tradition of libertarianism in the organisation's decisions and policies.

Robertson, James C., *The Hidden Cinema. British Film Censorship in Action 1913-1972,* London, Routledge, 1989.
Robertson offers a series of detailed case histories of films submitted to the BBFC between these years and the focus is again on the social and historical contexts of the films and the BBFC decisions, rather than on a reading of the films themselves. A very useful source of information on individual films, although Robertson does not mention video, despite the fact that many of the historical films he refers to have been submitted on video to the BBFC since 1984 and are now in distribution.

Schumach, Murray, *The Face on the Cutting Room Floor: The Story of Movie and Television Censorship,* New York, William Morrow and Co., 1964.
Very readable history of censorship in the United States taking in The Hays Code and the Hollywood 'blacklists' (the effects of which were still being felt as the book was written). It also predates the current American ratings system and offers a valuable perspective on the focus for and against allowing nudity in American films in the early 1960s.

Trevelyan, John, *What the Censor Saw,* London, Michael Joseph, 1973.
A personal account by the 60s film censor of his work as Secretary of the BBFC, which is part professional autobiography, part social history and, at the end, part polemic for an end to film censorship for adults.

(Read together, Phelps and Trevelyan offer a remarkably detailed account of film censorship in the 60s and 70s.)

Wistrich, Enid, *I don't mind the sex, it's the violence,* London, Calder, 1976.
Along with Phelps and Trevelyan, Wistrich engages with the 'censorship debate' of the 70s. As head of the then Greater London Council Film Viewing Board from 1973 to 1975, Wistrich reached firm anti-censorship conclusions which she outlines here. The book also indicates the relationship between the local authorities and the BBFC – the GLC viewing fifteen or so controversial films a year in the early 70s compared to the three to four hundred annually viewed by the BBFC.

B   Related books on paternal and social media regulation

Barker, Martin, *A Haunt of Fears, The Strange History of the British Horror Comics Campaign,* London, Pluto, 1984.
Barker looks at the pressure groups whose campaign against imported American 'horror comics' in the 50s led to the passing of The Children and Young Persons (Harmful Publications) Act 1958, which is still in force. He then also offers textual readings of some reproduced comic strips.

Sutherland, John, *Offensive Literature, Decensorship in Britain 1960-1982,* London, Junction Books, 1982.
An account of famous prosecutions of literature under the Obscene Publications Act and other laws relating to censorship – covering among others the *Lady Chatterley's Lover* trial and the prosecution of William Burroughs's *The Naked Lunch.* Sutherland offers an extremely useful overview of the findings of the Williams Report.

C   Sources of information on the classification of film and video in the present

Ferman, James, *BBFC Annual Reports* 1985-present. Copies can be purchased from:
The British Board of Film Classification
3 Soho Square
London W1V 5DE

Ferman, James, Obscenity, Manners and Morals in the Media, in Hoggart, Richard (ed.), *Liberty and Legislation,* London, Frank Cass & Co Ltd, 1989, pp. 47-76.
Many interviews, press reports, etc. can be found about film and video censorship in the 80s and 90s. This is the most detailed and useful exposition of the current Board's understanding and application of obscenity legislation in relation to adult censorship.

James, Derek and Platt, Steve, *Banned!,* London, BFI, 1991.
A series of articles published in booklet form by the BFI, *New Statesmen and Society* and Channel Four television to accompany its censorship season of films and programmes transmitted in April 1991. Contains some productive articles for classroom discussion but also contains factual inaccuracies.

D   The following books of British film history refer to film censorship as part of their overview

Chanan, Michael, *The Dream that Kicks – The Prehistory and Early Years of Cinema in Britain,* London, Routledge & Kegan Paul, 1980. Chanan covers the early years of British cinema and touches on the social and historical conditions for the appearance of film censorship.

Hill, John, *Sex, Class and Realism: British Cinema 1951-63,* London, BFI, 1986.
Discusses the British social realist films of the late 50s early 1960s and touches on the significance of the 'X' certificates in the marketing and the reception of films like *Room at the Top* (1959).

Low, Rachael, *The History of the British Film* (3 vols.), London, Allen & Unwin, 1968.

Walker, Alexander, *Hollywood England. The British Film Industry in the Sixties,* London, Michael Joseph, 1974; and Walker, Alexander, *National Heroes. British Cinema in the Seventies and Eighties,* London, Harveys, 1982.

Both have frequent references to film censorship and the BBFC.

E   Other source material used in this guide

Bowker, Julian (ed.), *Secondary Media Education: A Curriculum Statement,* London, BFI, 1991.

Ellis, John, *Visible Fictions,* London, Routledge & Kegan Paul, 1982.

Greene, Graham, *The Pleasure Dome, The Collected Film Criticism 1935-1940,* Oxford, OUP, 1980.

Thompson, Hunter S., *Hell's Angels,* London, Penguin, 1967.

PART THREE
TEACHING MATERIALS

Contents

This section comprises materials for use in the classroom. These materials are arranged in eight sections, each section corresponding to an aspect of film and video censorship and classification.

1   Preliminary work: audiences

Introduction

The restriction of access to cinemas to certain age groups and the declaring illegal of the process of renting or buying videos by them according to the contents of film and video material, relies not only on a set of judgments about how this material addresses audiences, but also about the way in which the audience's reading of the film and video material is partially determined by its age and the range of experiences it can call upon. To stimulate students to start thinking critically about both sides of this equation, about both the varying bases for the judgments made in relation to the evidence of the material itself (the reading of the individual film and video texts on the part of the classification authority) and considerations around the question of audiences and age, it is useful to begin with the latter. Work may have been done on the question of media audiences in media education lower down the school, in which case the specific considerations to be raised in the classroom activities and discussion proposed in this section can build on the knowledge and skills already developed.

The initial aim is to encourage the students' view of themselves as an audience (or audiences) which is active in the making of decisions before and during the consumption of film in the cinema or at home or elsewhere on video. This should help students begin to reflect on how age, as one factor in their self-definition as an audience, affects their tastes, expectations and their viewing habits. How, for example, does age as a factor compare with gender, as another aspect which could affect how an audience is defined by others (producers, advertisers, those responsible for the marketing of the film or video product) and can define itself? Is a fifteen-year-old female likely to have more or less in common, when it comes to preferred viewing, with a twelve- or eighteen-year-old of the same gender or a male of her own age, for example?

Activities 1, 2 and 3 prepare students for thinking about the broader institutional and audience contexts of each of the case studies. They are designed to be introduced in order, each building on the knowledge and experience of the other. However, you may wish to be selective according to the depth of detail you require.

The preliminary suggestions aim to provide ways of starting to think about general issues of 'restrictions of young people's behaviour under the law', what films and videos they watch and what knowledge they have about the classification process.

Using the materials

Organising a typical programme of work using these materials could usefully start with some or all the introductory activities 1-4 and proceed onto any one of the sections 2, 3 and 4, based on a historical example dealing with representations of youth and themes of violence, or sexual imagery and young audiences. One might adapt particular units, independently. For example, to explore the importance of viewing contexts on audience reception one might select section 7, 'Viewing contexts'.

It is advised that work be organised selectively, conceptually or thematically – it is unlikely that any programme of work would cover all of the sections.

Background and commentary

Background information from any of the three Parts could be used as course reading in preparation for discussion or essay writing. It is anticipated that the material will be photocopied and circulated for this purpose.

From Part One students could familiarise themselves with typical features of 'debates' about effects and classification and censorship. From Part Two students can glean particulars about the history and role of the BBFC throughout its development. The prefaces and notes of various sections of Part Three contain background information about the case studies. There are also introductory commentaries describing particular features of teaching and learning about each thematic area.

Teaching approaches

Before starting the activities it is worth briefly highlighting three distinct models of teaching about institutions so as to hold up the magnifying glass to the question of how media studies students might learn most effectively.

One model is to start with textual analysis and work towards institutional and ideological issues by exploring how and why the text is influenced by factors not visible in the text itself. In this instance, reading of the background introductory sections to this pack may be deferred till later. A second model starts with the context in which the texts are produced: a sociological approach studies the organisation and structures of media-related institutions and their relationship to the state, monopoly, capitalism, etc. In this model, knowledge about historical and social structures and political processes is gained before tackling the texts themselves. A third model relates to student production itself. In this model, the emphasis is placed on student reflection on the processes and products of their own and team-based production of media texts. For instance, they might have a brief which includes dealing with a contentious element, especially given the audiences for whom the text is targeted. In the production-led learning environment, understanding and knowledge is achieved by students reflecting on the detail and experience of the decision-making and the creative, social and group dynamics and processes which characterise their media production team – an approximated though not actual microcosm of organisational and institutional practice.

Clearly, each of these models provides something which the others do not, and from these and other models teachers will make their own cocktail or undiluted potion. The model inherent in the material which follows aims to provide opportunities for all three models to be blended, with the third model being less prominent. Here, the subject of a production-led approach is most likely to result from local circumstances.

It is this book's premise that the interdependent media concepts outlined in Part One, 'Teaching about Film and Video Censorship and Classification', will underpin any model of learning or teaching.

Activity 1 Questionnaire and survey

Aims

- To promote a critical appraisal by the students of their own viewing habits by encouraging them to examine the ways in which they select and consume the media texts for which they form an audience.
- To introduce the students to the process of gathering the type of empirical information which is often used to form the basis for discussion of media 'effects' and audience attitudes.

Objectives

Students will be expected to develop and demonstrate

- skill in gathering information for media audiences and 'effects' research;
- an understanding of the ways in which information about media audiences and 'effects' can be analysed and discussed.

You will need

Activity Sheet 1 (p. 37-38), the questionnaire. You may prefer to ask students to devise their own questionnaires (see Notes).

What you do

Hand out copies of the questionnaire. Split the students into small groups to compare samples of the completed sheets. You may like to complete a questionnaire yourself (see Notes). In discussing and analysing the results focus the students' attention on the following areas of enquiry:

- In what circumstances do people watch films and videos?
- How do people choose what they watch?
- What do people think about what they watch?
- How is age related to the above questions and what other factors apply?

- What role, if any, do the BBFC classifications play in what is watched and how it is watched?

Follow-up activities

Widen the scope of the survey to a cross-section of students in the same year as the group and then among older and younger pupils. Initially, for comparison, students could call upon older friends, relatives, parents or guardians to take part in order to widen the range of data from the point of view of the age of respondents. The questionnaire on Activity Sheet 1 will have to be modified slightly for this part of the exercise.

Once the students have gathered their data from the questionnaires, it can be analysed to see if it suggests any correlation between modes of film and video viewing and age. Do they think younger teenagers watch more or fewer videos than older ones? Are older adults likely to watch different films and videos? Does the gender of viewers have more or less of an effect on what they watch and how they watch it as they get older? The students' assumptions and observations about these and other questions suggested by the aims of the questionnaire can then be compared with the results, and the factors affecting this can also be discussed.

As film and video classification into age categories is a practice which effectively seeks to ban material for certain audiences it might be assumed that young people under the ages of fifteen and eighteen, the ages stipulated by the two prohibitive categories, are more aware of the classification of videos and films than older people or their parents. Is this borne out by the results of the survey?

Notes

The questionnaire is based on one which was devised for use in a number of schools in London in 1991-2 by the BBFC and as part of a series of classroom discussions about censorship and classification.

It introduces the students to the kind of audience survey, market research and social science research methods, which have been used as the basis for discussion of audiences and 'effects'. One of the problems with employing this exercise in relation to media education classroom work using censorship and classification as a topic, is that there is always the danger that pupils will feel that their private viewing is being 'policed' in some way by their teacher, and that the subtext to such a survey is a kind of 'checking up' on the students' activities outside the classroom, rather than the genuine aim of using the existing viewing practices of the students to yield valid knowledge which can help promote critical thought. This is, of course, not an unreasonable conclusion for the students to reach given that a good deal of social science research into the possibility of detrimental effects of viewing certain material is often based in value judgments about the material itself. The National Viewers' Survey which was produced in 1984 by academics and church groups and the NSPCC (see Part Two, p. 23) set out to establish that a large number of children had seen violent videos, with the implications of the findings having been largely prejudged. The point of encouraging the students in this context, and in sharp distinction to surveys which are motivated by an explicit 'concern' over children's and young people's viewing, is that the students can discover the problems inherent in such surveys by conducting one themselves, and by discussing the results of this activity in classroom groups.

The questionnaire is by no means intended to be a model of its kind. Given the problem just described, the teacher may prefer to have the students discuss and then devise their own questionnaire. This approach has the added benefit of encouraging the students to think right from the outset about the kind of areas of enquiry relevant to questions of age, audience and regulation.

Questionnaire

1. How many TVs are there in your house?

   0   1   2   3+   (ring one number)

2. How many video recorders are there in your house?

   0   1   2   3+   (ring one number)

3. Roughly how many films have you seen at the cinema in the last month?
   What titles can you remember of these?

4. Who did you go with? Tick as many as apply.

   · Parent(s)/Guardian(s)   _____
   Brother(s)/Sister(s)   _____
   Boyfriend or Girlfriend   _____
   Other Friends   _____
   Other Relatives   _____
   Alone   _____
   Other (please specify)   _____

5. Roughly how many films have you watched on video in the last couple of weeks? (Don't include any films recorded off TV.)
   What titles can you remember?

6. Who did you watch them with?

   Parent(s)/Guardian(s)   _____
   Brother(s)/Sister(s)   _____
   Boyfriend or Girlfriend   _____

   Other Friends   _____
   Other Relatives   _____
   Alone   _____
   Other (please specify)   _____

7. Who chooses the tapes usually?

8. Who usually pays when you go to the cinema?

9. Who usually pays when you rent a video?

10. What TV programmes did you watch last night?

11. Roughly how long did you watch all together?

12. Who were you mostly watching with?

    Parent(s)/Guardian(s)   _____
    Brother(s)/Sister(s)   _____
    Boyfriend or Girlfriend   _____
    Other Friends   _____
    Other Relatives   _____
    Alone   _____
    Other (please specify)   _____

13. Who chooses which programmes to watch?

14. Are there any differences between the videos that you see at home and the videos you see at friends' houses?

    No   _____
    Yes   _____   (please specify)

15. What TV programmes did you watch last weekend?

16. Roughly how long did you watch on Saturday?

Roughly how long did you watch on Sunday?

17. Who were you mostly watching with at the weekend?

Parent(s)/Guardian(s) _____
Brother(s)/Sister(s) _____
Boyfriend or Girlfriend _____
Other Friends _____
Other Relatives _____
Alone _____
Other (please specify) _____

18. Who mostly chooses the programmes to watch?

Parent(s)/Guardian(s) _____
Brother(s)/Sister(s) _____
Boyfriend or Girlfriend _____
Other Friends _____
Other Relatives _____
You _____
Other (please specify) _____

19. Do your parents have any rules or agreements about what you watch on TV?

No _____
Yes _____ (What are these?)

20. Do your parents have any rules or agreements about what you watch on video?

21. What are your favourite TV programmes at the moment?

22. What are the films that you like best that you have seen recently at the cinema or on video?

23. Do you prefer watching at the cinema or at home?

Cinema _____
Home _____

24. Write down as many of the film categories that apply in the cinema as you can remember.

25. Write down as many of the categories that apply on video as you can remember.

26. Do you think that there is too much ...

	Yes	No	Don't know No opinion
sex on TV	—	—	—
violence on TV	—	—	—
bad language on TV	—	—	—
sex on video	—	—	—
violence on video	—	—	—
bad language on video	—	—	—

27. Do you think your parent(s)/guardian(s) have any views on the above question?

No _____
Yes _____ (What are these views?)

My age is _____
I am male _____ female _____

Activity 2 Viewing diary

Aims

- To encourage the students to think about the modes of address of the media texts with which they come into contact and how considerations of suitability for specific age groups relate to them.
- To promote a discussion of how decisions about suitability taken by regulators relate to their own viewing habits and opinions.

Objective

- Students should develop an awareness of the process of categorisation for age groups, either through the age categories used by the BBFC for films and videos or through placing in the television schedules, or from advice in newspapers, television listings, magazines, etc.

You will need

Activity Sheet 2 (p. 40) containing a blank page for a viewing diary. The students should be encouraged to bring in other material connected to the texts they have viewed which they may have used as a source for their comments on the texts' intended suitability.

What you do

The students should be instructed to keep the diary for a week or more. It is most likely, if the diary is kept for a relatively short period of time that the films (or television programmes) will have been viewed on television rather than on video or in the cinema.

The completed diaries can be compared and discussed with the students working in small groups.

Notes

The students should not, of course, take this activity as an instruction to go away and watch (or for young students to prevail upon their parents to let them watch) what they may consider to be unsuitable material. The aim is for the students to follow their usual viewing habits and to begin to think about how notions of suitability for intended audiences may have informed aspects of the production, scheduling or classification of the texts they have viewed.

You may also find it useful to photocopy and distribute the sheet containing the current BBFC category symbols in Part Two (p. 48). As a follow-up activity and part of the discussion of the viewing diaries, it may be useful to have the students describe, from their own experiences or opinions, what they would expect of films or videos falling into each of the categories.

This diary should be used to keep a record of the films you watch in the cinema, on video or on television or of any television programmes you watch. If applicable you should make a note of the classification given to the film, why you think it was given that classification, or who you think the programme was suitable for or unsuitable for. For programmes on broadcast television or satellite and cable, you should also note the date and time of transmission.

FILM/PROGRAMME TITLE	REASON	CLASSIFICATION AND/ OR AGE FOR WHICH YOU FELT IT WAS SUITABLE/UNSUITABLE
DATE:		
DATE:		
DATE:		
DATE:		

Activity 3 Classroom discussion: audiences, age and the law

Introduction

In order for the students to begin to examine their own ideas and opinions about the regulation of media texts, about censorship and classification, it is important that they recognise that these ideas and opinions are based on assumptions about how young people and adults view media texts and the role that media texts play in the lives and experiences of people of different ages.

Against this, it is also important for the students to appreciate that media regulation, particularly in its traditional form of age bars at the cinema box office, exists as one aspect of the way an individual's progress to adulthood is defined by regulations and legislation aimed at protecting children from harmful experiences or for responsibilities for which they are not yet ready.

Aim

- To expand this initial discussion of classification of media texts by audience age groups to include more general classroom discussion of media classification and censorship.

Objectives

To allow the student to identify and investigate:

- her/his own attitudes and assumptions about institutional film and video classification and censorship of media texts;
- the institutional, familial and legal media contexts for discussion of classification and suitability.

You will need

The list of statements in Activity Sheet 3a (p. 42).
Activity Sheet 3b, 'How old do you have to be?' (p. 43-4).
Activity Sheet 3c (p. 45).

What you do

Distribute photocopies of Activity Sheet 3a to the students and ask them in small groups to arrange the statements in the order which best reflects their own views. It may be useful to copy the statements onto cards which the groups can rearrange during their discussion of the merits of the individual statements. The students should then be asked to justify and explain their ranking of these statements. Discussion should then focus on any differences between the conclusions of the groups.

The various legal considerations listed on Activity Sheet 3b can be introduced into the discussion at the teacher's discretion. How does the regulation of media texts compare with other forms of regulation protecting or affecting young people and children? Are there useful comparisons to be made, for example, between media regulation and legal restraints on the purchase of alcohol or cigarettes, for example? (The representation of drink in advertising forms the basis of Activity 14 (p. 110) later in the workbook.)

Introduce Activity Sheet 3c. Discuss the differences in age levels, and comment on what factors make the different countries organise the levels as they have done. Some European countries distinguish between age levels to give parents guidance. Others leave the judgment up to parents as long as they accompany the children.

STATEMENTS

A   Films and videos can affect the way people think about themselves and other people.

B   People don't take films seriously because films are just for entertainment.

C   Children ignore those bits of films they don't understand.

D   Children can be very upset by what they see in films and on video.

E   Children and young people are able to choose their own viewing.

F   Parents know more about videos and films than their children.

G   I get embarrassed if I am watching a video with my family and there is a sex scene/bad language/too much violence.

H   I am mature enough to decide what films or videos to see but I wouldn't want my younger brother/sister/anybody younger than me to watch some things.

I   I would rather see a '15' certificate video or film because it is more likely to be exciting or interesting than one classified as a 'PG' or 'U'.

J   I prefer to see films about people of my age group.

K   It is more fun to watch videos with friends than on my own.

L   Videos and films can teach people how to commit crimes.

M   Older people are less impressionable than younger people.

N   Most films are made for younger people and sometimes older people don't understand them.

O   People are more likely to get upset by films if they only rarely go to the cinema or watch videos.

How old do you have to be?

AGE

At birth	A bank or building society account can be opened in the child's name and he/she can own premium bonds.
6 weeks	The child can be handed to prospective adopters.
$4\frac{1}{2}$ mths	The child can be adopted.
2	The child can join a nursery school.
3	The child must be paid for on public transport.
5	The child must receive full-time education and can drink alcohol in private.
7	The child can draw money from a TSB or PO savings account.
10	The child can be found guilty of a crime if it can be shown that he/she knew it was wrong – maximum £100.
12	The child can buy a pet.
13	The child can open a current account at a bank at the discretion of the bank manager.
14	The child can take a part-time job; can be found guilty of a criminal offence as if an adult (although the mode of trial and the sentence will be different); can be fined up to £400 and sent to a detention centre (if male); must pay full fare on British Rail; can own an airgun; can go into a bar with an adult but cannot consume an alcoholic drink; a boy can be found guilty of rape and unlawful intercourse with a girl under sixteen; the police can take the child's finger and palm prints.
15	The child can own a shotgun and ammunition; can be sent to youth custody; can be admitted to a film rated '15'.

16 The child can marry if there is parental consent; can apply for supplementary benefit in his/her own right; can buy fireworks; can consent to medical treatment and choose his/her own doctor; can leave school and then work full time; can buy a ticket in a registered public lottery; can join a trade union; can drink beer, cider, porter or sherry in a pub, but only with a meal in a part of the pub that serves meals, not at the bar; can drive a moped or tractor; can fly solo in a glider; can buy cigarettes (he/she can smoke at any age); has to pay prescription charges; has to pay the full fare on buses and on the Underground; a boy can join the armed forces, with parental consent; a girl can consent to sexual intercourse.

$16\frac{1}{2}$ The child can receive sickness and unemployment benefit.

17 The child can drive a car or motorcycle; can go into a betting shop (but not bet); can have an airgun in a public place; can fly a plane solo; can be tried on any charge in an adult court; a girl can join the armed forces, with parental consent.

18 The child becomes an adult and can vote; can sue in his/her own name; can marry without parental consent; can change his/her name; can apply for a passport; can own land (including a house); can enter into binding contracts; can obtain credit (including HP) and have a cheque or credit card; can be eligible for jury service; can buy drinks in the bar of a pub; can be tattooed; can donate blood and organs; can bet; can make a will; can join the armed forces without parental consent; can be admitted to a film rated '18'; a male can consent to sexual intercourse with another male.

21 The adult can now stand in a general or local election; can apply for a liquor licence; can drive a lorry or a bus; can be sent to prison.

European Film Categories

For all	Denmark	France	Germany	Iceland	Ireland	Netherlands
('U')	Spain	Sweden	Belgium	UK	Norway (under 5 accompanied)	
'Uc'	UK					
'4'	Portugal					
'5'	Norway					
'6'	Germany	Portugal				
'PG'	UK					
NRC 7	Denmark	Spain				
'7'	Sweden					
'10'	Iceland	Norway (5-10 accompanied)				
'11'	Sweden					
'12A'	Ireland (under 12 accompanied)					
'12'	Denmark	France	Germany	Iceland	Portugal	UK
'NRC 13'	Spain					
'15'	Norway	Sweden	Ireland	UK		
'16'	Denmark	France	Germany	Iceland	Netherlands	Portugal
	Belgium					
'NRC 18'	Spain					
'18'	Germany	Ireland	Norway	Portugal	UK	Sweden (planned)
'18X' ('R18')	France	Portugal	Spain	UK	Netherlands	

KEY:

Uc	=	Unaccompanied by adults
PG	=	Parental guidance
NRC	=	Not recommended for children
R18	=	Restricted '18' licensed sex cinemas or cinemas with sex shops. It is a category which the countries use to 'zone' pornography

How do European film categories differ from those in Britain?

What factors do you think decide these categories (e.g. with parents of unaccompanied children)?

Activity 4 Investigating the role of the BBFC

Aim

- To investigate the history and to identify the function of the BBFC and its role as the British institutional regulator for the classification of film and video.

Objectives

To enable students to:

- become informed about the structure, history, legal status and role of the BBFC;
- understand the relationship between the regulatory institution, public debate about values, and the audiences of the media texts.

You will need

The background text from Part Two, 'A Brief Historical Account of Film and Video Censorship and Classification in Britain' (p. 11), video clip 1, Gwyneth Cook's interview with Margaret Ford, Deputy Director of the BBFC, and film director, Michael Winner and video clip 2 which includes Barry Norman's interview with James Ferman, Director of the BBFC.

What you do

How much information you wish to introduce at this stage depends on how much is already known about the BBFC. The information in Part Two could be read and discussed in relation to general knowledge about *causes célèbres* or particular texts. Issues about the role of the state, the Church, the family and the media in public debate could be introduced to set the overall context of institutional roles and ideological processes.

For general familiarisation with the Board's activities, the video clips of James Ferman and Margaret Ford provide a useful starting point for exploring the question, 'What is the BBFC and what is its purpose and role?'

Notes

Background to BBFC examiners – who are they? The BBFC employs examiners who are familiar with:

- children and young people (teachers, social workers, parents);
- the law (magistrates);
- current debates in public life; and
- display an ability to interpret films and convey their individual readings verbally and can appreciate the possible meanings of different kinds of film and video from popular culture to European art films.

These requirements mean that the BBFC is staffed by examiners who are:

- educated to a certain level, so are more likely, for example, to be middle class than working class (although this is not uniformly the case in practice);
- older than the cinema audience – the youngest ever examiner at the BBFC (the author of the present guide) was twenty-seven when he became an examiner.

Mostly examiners are in their thirties or forties. The BBFC is made up equally of men and women examiners, and they are drawn from a number of ethnic groups – staffing is in proportion to the type of material submitted. There is currently a provision for one examiner for Cantonese films and one for Hindi films.*

The Director is appointed by the Home Office and a board of governors is drawn from a range of public and commercial sectors. The film industry regulates itself through this structure with the Director at its head.

Follow-up activity

As an additional activity students could discuss the different audiences and how issues of censorship were involved when the programme producers included clips with these interviews. *Going Live* was broadcast between 9 a.m. and 12 p.m. on a Saturday morning, and *Film 92* was broadcast between 10.30 p.m. and 11.30 p.m. on a weekday.

Give students the following brief: using any of the interview footage in *Going Live* or *Film 92,* what clips, from films you have watched, would you use for a programme called *Moviewatch*, broadcast on Channel Four at 6 p.m. on Friday evenings, aimed at under-twenty-fives. Remember the programmer has to observe a sensitivity to the types of audiences watching television at this time. The 'family' viewing time is usually constructed as finishing around 9 p.m. in what is known as the 'watershed', the period between family and adult viewing.

At this stage, it may be considered convenient to establish ground rules for how the student group talks about issues which may be difficult for some and tolerated by others. For example, American and European audiences find it curious that British audiences tend to put 'bad language' so high on the agenda.

*Foreign language videos

The proportion of videos classified in the untranslated languages of Britain's various ethnic minorities has been in decline in recent years, from nearly a third of the total in 1989 to only 19 per cent in 1991. In 1992, it dropped even further, to 13.6 per cent, most of the fall being accounted for by dwindling submissions in the two major languages, Hindi and Cantonese, in each of which some distributors have ceased submitting to the Board. It is possible that the recession is taking its toll of some of the smaller ethnic distributors, but there are clearly others who prefer to operate outside the system.

Languages covered by the Board for classification are: Arabic, Bengali, Cantonese, Greek, Gujarati, Haryavni, Hindi, Mandarin, Punjabi, Tamil, Turkish, Urdu. (Information from BBFC Annual Report for 1992.)

BRITISH BOARD OF FILM CLASSIFICATION

CERTIFICATION SYMBOLS
FOR VIDEO PACKAGING AND PUBLICITY

Symbols only, for use on:

1) Cassettes: front and spine of case and top and spine of spool

2) Discs: front of disc sleeve and centre of disc itself

Symbol plus explanatory statement for use on:

1) Cassettes: reverse side of case

2) Discs: reverse side of sleeve

UNIVERSAL
Suitable for all

UNIVERSAL
Particularly suitable
for children

PARENTAL GUIDANCE
General viewing, but some
scenes may be unsuitable
for young children

Suitable only for
persons of
15 years and over

Not to be supplied to any person below that age

Suitable only for
persons of
18 years and over

Not to be supplied to any person below that age

RESTRICTED. To be supplied
only in licensed sex shops
to persons of
not less than 18 years

PRINTER'S COLOUR REFERENCE: **RED**: 80% YELLOW + 100% MAGENTA. **YELLOW**: 100% YELLOW. **BLUE**: 100% CYAN + 30% MAGENTA. **GREEN**: 100% CYAN + 40% MAGENTA. **GREEN**: YELLOW + 100% CYAN.

2 Historical example of film censorship: *The Wild One* (US, Laslo Benedek, 1953)

Introduction

This section contains material for classroom activities on film censorship, using one famous example of film censorship as a basis. The information and activities are organised around promoting in the students a critical understanding of:

- the importance of social and historical contexts in the way films produce meanings for different audiences;
- the way these meanings may change with shifting contexts and the passage of time;
- the way in which the circulation of meanings of a media text can also be constructed by critics, newspaper reports and publicity;
- the complex ways in which film texts relate to real events and social concerns.

Background

The Wild One was made in the United States in 1953 and banned the following year for British audiences by the BBFC. It remained banned, having only been shown by film societies and in parts of the country where the local authorities had overturned the BBFC's decision, until 1967, when it was finally released with a BBFC 'X' certificate. It was passed 'PG' on video in 1988.

The BBFC being a much smaller organisation in the 50s than it is today, decisions on controversial material were made by discussion between the censors (the Secretary and the President) and the two to four part time examiners employed by them. Today, in the case of controversial films, the Director and if necessary the Presidential tier make the decision with reference to a wide range of reports from advisory part-time examiners. This means that no reports exist in the BBFC files to indicate any range of opinion on the film. The Secretary of the Board, Arthur Watkins, described the reasons for the decision in letters to local authorities, who had to decide whether to ratify this decision, and representatives of the distribution company, Columbia Pictures, as well as in response to enquiries from members of the public. This letter is reproduced in Information Sheet 1 (p. 50).

Attempts to change the narrative of the film

During the rest of 1954, various informal appeals were made to the BBFC by Columbia Pictures, who were concerned that a film starring Marlon Brando, a very successful star following his appearance in *A Streetcar Named Desire* (US, Elia Kazan, 1951) and *On the Waterfront* (US, Elia Kazan, 1954), should be denied its share of British box-office takings. As the BBFC is an industry body which had throughout its history attempted to solve 'problems' like those presented by *The Wild One* by cutting out the elements of which it disapproved, rather than outright banning, the distributor set out to prove that this course of action should have been taken in this case by suggesting over thirty re-edits in order, in the words of the Columbia official who devised them, to 'contribute much in the way of affirmative values' to the film. This meant a reorganisation of the film so that depictions of 'disrespect for the law, vandalism and unnecessary violence' were removed. Examples of the cuts suggested by the company are reproduced on Information Sheet 2 (p. 51).

These changes, although clearly taking their cue from some of the objections expressed by the BBFC, evidently failed to make the film's perspective on 'juvenile delinquency' any more acceptable to the censors, who felt that a social problem had still been transformed into a spectacle:

> As far as we are concerned, it is in all essentials the film we have already seen so many times and concerning which our views have been made so clear. A foreword has been tagged on a number of dialogue cuts which have been made – almost all relating to the character of the police officer ... and a new, and to our minds wholly unconvincing ending has been

The Town Clerk
City Council Chambers
Clarence Parade
Portsmouth   19th April, 1955

Dear Sir

The Wild One was first viewed by the Board on the 18th January 1954 and the Company were informed that the Board was not prepared to issue a certificate in any category. In response to representations made by the Distributors, the film was viewed again on 8th December 1954, and, after the most careful consideration, the Company were informed that the Board was unable to reverse its previous decision.

The film deals with organised hooliganism and deliberate outrage of all law and order by a group of young toughs who at weekends ride about the countryside on motorcycles under an acknowledged leader. The story is said to be based on an actual incident in the United States which emphasises the seriousness of all that happens, and the happenings include a long series of unprovoked insults and attacks on young and old alike in a small town, looting and destruction of property in a wild orgy, and finally the death of an innocent old man. The local police officer is helpless and ineffective and his daughter against her better nature 'falls for' the leader of the gang, demonstrating the morbid attraction which such young toughs can have for immature girls. When police reinforcements finally appear, the youths are allowed to get away with a mild and quite inadequate caution and so made to appear rather clever fellows than silly and dangerous young fools.

The behaviour of similar rowdy gangs of youths in our large towns is, as you are aware, a matter of serious concern to the police in this country and public opinion has been strongly aroused by several incidents which have occurred here since the end of the war. The Board regards it as of the utmost importance to ensure that no film it certificates shall, through exercising the wrong kind of influence on young people, aggravate this and, above all, a film whose subject is irresponsible juvenile behaviour. The issue of a certificate by the Board to *The Wild One* would throw the film open – even with the safeguard of the 'X' category – to those very youths between the ages of 16 and 20 who constitute the problem of juvenile delinquency. The Board believes that the influence on that age group would be dangerous in the extreme, since the hooliganism in the film, unresisted and in the end virtually unpunished, would be likely to compel their admiration rather than their censure.

(Letter from Arthur Watkins to Portsmouth County Council. BBFC records.)

submitted by the video distribution company, RCA Columbia, in 1986 and viewed as a new submission. It was the view of the examiners that the film was a period piece on video and eventually, when the video was classified in 1988, the year by which the backlog of videos which needed classifying had to be certificated, the video was passed 'PG' by the Board's Director. *The Wild One* has also been transmitted in its original version on network television, most recently as part of a 50s film season on Channel Four during Christmas 1991. An example of an examiner's report on *The Wild One*, 1986 is on p. 57.

Introducing discussion of *The Wild One* in the classroom
In John Trevelyan's account of his time as Secretary of the BBFC, *What the Censor Saw*, he encapsulated the issues raised by the film for censors:

> In 1954, when I was a part-time examiner, we had a film of some brilliance which caused us concern – this was *The Wild One* in which Marlon Brando gave a magnetic performance. We decided that we must refuse a certificate, not really on the grounds of its violence as it is usually stated, but because of its message. The film showed a gang of motorcycle thugs terrorising a small town. It was, in fact, based on a real incident. It showed how authority became scared and therefore weak and suggested that if there were enough hoodlums and they behaved in a menacing way, they could get away with it. This was at a time when the activities of what were called 'Teddy Boys' were beginning to cause concern. We felt that in this film was a danger of stimulation and imitation. (Trevelyan, 1973, p. 152.)

Rather than discussing in class the rights and wrongs of banning *The Wild One* in the 50s – probably a very short debate as it is unlikely that any member of the class would see this film as controversial – it is productive to discuss the rationale for censorship of films addressing young people. See also video clips 1 and 2 with members of the Board discussing their rationales. This rationale relates to:

- the 'message' of the film;
- what this message conveys about recognisable social problems and/or events in the real world connected with social problems;
- the possibility that the film will cause audiences to imitate the behaviour represented and therefore be seen to be exacerbating social problems.

This rationale is, then, not overtly concerned with the question of an audience being shocked, offended or disgusted, although this may be the response of sections of the audience who react in these ways to films which appear to them to be conveying 'anti-social messages'. It is a moral welfare argument which bases itself in the idea that films can affect the way suitably disposed audiences view the world and their place within it, and that this process can be one contributory factor resulting in criminal behaviour. This view that films can have such direct and predictable effects in this way is far from being a universally accepted one. The usefulness of looking at the way *The Wild One* can be read against this rationale is that it can provoke critical thought on the students' part about the notion that films can have identifiable 'messages'. Do people read these 'messages' in the same way? Were the censors worried about one particular reading? By one particular audience?

Fear of imitation: censorship arguments
It is important to realise that although *The Wild One* is now uncontroversial for censors and, presumably, most viewers, the reasons why this should be the case can also be the focus of classroom discussion about the different elements which make up the 'messages' the viewer takes from a film – the rationale for the censor's concern remains in place and affects the BBFC's treatment of videos and films today. A

Films and Filming, June 1955

THE WILD ONE

Directed by Laslo Benedek. Produced by Stanley Kramer. Script by John Paxton. Music by Leith Stevens. Photography by Hal Moore, ASC. Edited by Al Clark. American. Columbia. 77 mins. Cert. X in certain areas.

Johnny — — — — — —	MARLON BRANDO
Kathy — — — — — —	MARY MURPHY
Town Marshal — — — —	ROBERT KEITH
Chief of Police — — — —	JAY C. FLIPPEN
Chino — — — — — —	LEE MARVIN

ONE day, perhaps, *The Wild One* may be brought out of musty vaults and viewed from the safe distance of history as a social document. It captures precisely the vicious irrationalism of the young thug gangs coughed up by our sick society in London, Paris and the cities of America. It presents one such gang and gives its point of view.

The line of the story is sordid and complicated. As a brilliant piece of direction, as a piece of fine photography, as a new example of powerful Brandonic acting, as a film which is, in fact, less brutal than *On the Waterfront*, *The Wild One* might have warranted the censor's certificate. But technical brilliance does not succeed in disguising the poisoned content as it does, perhaps, in *On the Waterfront*. The censor, no doubt, refused it a certificate on moral grounds because, as a journalist friend remarked to me, "any young hooligan who sees this film will leave it with his morale two hundred per cent higher."

This, then, must be the point of judgment. Brando's acting is so powerful, the direction of the film so taut that the film wins our sympathy entirely for Johnny, for hooliganism. *The Wild One* meets violence with violence, savagery with savagery, evil with evil. It makes the people of the town as corrupt and vicious as the hooligans who rouse them to action. Kathy, the town marshal's daughter, alone has tenderness and warmth; apart from her there is nothing noble, generous or fine on the screen.

If this is a truthful or even partly truthful picture of America today the implications are sinister. The two groups of people who make war on each other—townsfolk and hooligans—are led by leaders who do the thinking for them, Johnny and Charlie, the bully shopkeeper who is a neighbour of the town marshal.

This kind of jungle society where might is right is the society I remember seeing in Germany before the war, the kind of thing one fought the war to destroy. The philosophy of this society is the philosophy of *The Wild One*.

The film never grasps or expresses the real tragedy of the boys, vigorous, gay, talented, who can find no other outlet for their creative energies than hooliganism. By its treatment it encourages their wrong way of living. It is never positive even in the way that *Nous sommes tous des assassins* (*Are we all Murderers?*) or *I Vitelloni* were positive. Its production cannot be justified solely on the grounds of "entertainment value." Although the opening titles say that "this can never happen again," the ending is so weak that one is left with more than a suspicion that its events are an interlude in the gang's activities and that they will continue all the stronger after coming almost unscathed through a first-class riot and a near manslaughter. **P.B.**

Dilys Powell review,
© The Sunday Times,
1 June 1955

THE CENSOR SAYS NO

By Dilys Powell

Unlike the Americans the British have no censorship code, no list of rules to be followed. But when the Board of Film Censors impose an X certificate they usually do so in the belief that the film is likely, sometimes to corrupt and frighten, but just as often to shake a child's faith in authority or in the ability of its parents to protect. *The Wild One* I assume was thought likely to corrupt or incite to violence audiences of the very age which with the X certificate can scrape into the cinema. Much though I admire the intellectual fury with which the film is made (and the liberality of the local authorities who permit its exhibition) I am bound to say I think the Board was absolutely right. ...

All the same I am glad to have seen it and not only because of its skill or the interest of the censor's decision. Eighteen years ago a reforming film called *Dead End* made a stir: it was a story of city streets and neglected boys with no outlet for the violent impulses of youth. *The Dead End* boys of today are the unpublished mob of *The Wild One*: dangerous boys on motor-bicycles, drumming along the roads with the savage intentness, and in something very like the uniform of Hitler's young thugs. In brutality the American film, I am afraid, has already come of age.

Alexander Walker review,
Evening Standard,
15 February 1968
© The source/Solo

BRANDO AND HIS LEATHER JACKETS:
AFTER FIFTEEN YEARS HOW
UN-VIOLENT IT ALL SEEMS

NEW FILMS
by ALEXANDER WALKER

FILM: The Wild One (Cert X).
Columbia.

STAR: Marlon Brando.

FEW films have sat on the shelf collecting dust while awaiting a West End showing as long as Marlon Brando's The Wild One. Fifteen years, in fact.

Made in 1953, its story of teenage motorcycle rowdies who take over and terrorise an American town was judged too much like an inflammation to imitation by our then film censor — who refused it a certificate.

Up to now it's had only spotty screenings in Britain under local council certificates or else in the cinema clubs. From today, all this changes.

The present censor, John Trevelyan, has decided the film can now be shown publicly—and safely. "Our own brand of rockers are now just a pre-historic race," he told me this week. "The film's dangerous appeal was aimed mainly at them." He could have added that today's teenagers are now tempted by the drugs kick, not the kick starter.

So see The Wild One—but prepare yourself for the surprises that the 15-year cooling-off period have created.

Surprise Number One is how un-violent it all seems now. Compared with the groin-punching, eye-gouging and karate-chopping that make up the bill at your friendly neighbourhood cinema these days, The Wild One is as bloody as a pillow fight.

It reminds us uneasily just how much physical brutality we've come to accept *as normal* in movies today.

Brando and his leather-jackets roar up Main Street in a flying wedge of wanton menace. By nightfall they've sealed the town off from SOS appeals. But they terrorise it not by violence so much as the latent threat in their sulky eyes and jeering cat-calls at the sheriff who tries to avoid trouble by ignoring it.

The only man to meet a violent death is the oldest inhabitant, and that's caused by the townsfolk whom the presence of the rowdies turn into a fascist gang of indignant bourgeoisie.

Even the beating-up they give Brando when they corner him alone leaves him hardly more bruised than a windfall apple. Compare it with the mangling he gets in a film like The Chase to see how the screen punch-up has escalated.

Nevertheless Surprise Number Two is Brando himself. As ever, he is a screen-holder.

His accent sounds like an impersonation of Jerry Lewis—high-pitched as a factory whistle, but oddly effective.

The Wild One was his fifth film, made aged 29, and immediately followed by his greatest success On The Waterfront. Familiar though his mannerisms already were—the lazy head-tilt, the eyes looking out at the world from some inner blockhouse of his being—we are jolted afresh by the way he's asked: "What are you rebelling against?" and spits out the line: "What have you got?"

But surprise Number Three is the most ironic one in the film.

For suddenly down the street on his motorcycle, in a pirate-striped vest, a hippy's beard, and with his muscled forearms tattooed like an obscene Popeye, roars Lee Marvin.

Then a small-part actor, he's now become the star of The Dirty Dozen and Point Blank. And as he and Brando have a sparring match, half in fun and half for real, we are reminded this is an encounter between one actor (Marvin) whose career has reached fruition just when that

SHOWDOWN ON MAIN STREET: THE THEN UNKNOWN LEE MARVIN TUSSLES WITH BRANDO.

of the other (Brando) has been rotting on the bough with a long run of indifferent movies.

Yes, you never know what will hit you—even after 15 years.

Synopsis

Johnny (Marlon Brando) and his large Black Rebels Motorcycle Club, ride into a small Western town after disrupting a motorcycle race and being ejected from the track where one of Johnny's friends steals a trophy for him. While the gang bides its time by 'dragging for beer' up and down the main street and drinking beer in Bleeker's bar, the townspeople react with confusion, greed and fear, and after an old man crashes his car due to the 'dragging', the ineffectual sheriff, Harry, refuses to take action. A tentative romance begins between Johnny and Harry's daughter Kathie and when Chino (Lee Marvin) arrives in town, a fight breaks out between him and Johnny over the stolen trophy, during which redneck bully Charley Thomas runs into one of the gang-members in his car. Harry arrests Johnny, which prompts the gang to take Charley from his house at night, cut the town's telephone connections, and replace Johnny with Charley in gaol. When Johnny saves Kathie from being tormented by his own gang, and takes her out of town, Kathie runs from him and the townspeople turn into vigilantes believing him to be attacking her. Johnny is knocked from his motorcycle, which kills an old man, and is beaten up by Charley Thomas and the vigilantes before being arrested by an out of town sheriff, who frees him after hearing that the accident was caused by the mob.

Comments

A censorship milestone on film, which was rejected in 1954 and first saw the light of day with a BBFC certificate in 1967 when John Trevelyan concluded that the style of the film's 'rebellious youths' and the cinematic techniques employed in their supposed glamorisation were no longer a threat to the fabric of British society. Although it is easy to mock the paternalistic considerations of the original censors, it would be unwise to consider the acceptability of *The Wild One* on film in the 60s, and the decision of the present examiners to pass it 'PG' on video, as being solely the product of a liberalisation of Board standards. In the light of many Hollywood films on the same subject since, *The Wild One* can now be recognised as a liberal statement against the mob mentality, as much of its time as *Twelve Angry Men* and *High Noon* and as a bittersweet love story which presents Brando from the opening voice-over as a traditional romantic hero rather than a 'dangerously' inviting icon of youth rebellion as he appeared at the time. It was the trappings of this statement that upset Arthur Watkins et al, and this imagery: leather jackets, motorcycles, rebellious styles in attitude, language, etc., have been colonised and muted by over 30 years of pop-culture and institutionalised commercial exploitation following the arrival of Rock and Roll, which, when the film was made, was merely a glimmer on the horizon. Like *Rebel Without a Cause*, this film is now both a historical document and family entertainment. Passed 'PG' without cuts.

(Examiner's Report, 1986)

Example of examiner's report on *The Wild One,* 1986

DISTRIBUTOR: DATE:

COUNTRY OF ORIGIN: CATEGORY: CUTS ☐   NO CUTS ☐

GENRE: REPORT BY:

ENGLISH LANGUAGE ☐   SUB-TITLED ☐   DUBBED ☐   FOR BOARD DISCUSSION ☐

APPROPRIATE CATEGORY:		Uc	U	PG	15	18	R18	CUTS	REJECT
THEME				✔		(✔)			
TREATMENT				✔					
VISUALS:	NUDITY								
	SEX								
	VIOLENCE			✔					
	HORROR								
LANGUAGE									
ALCOHOL					(✔)				
CRIMINAL TECHNIQUES									
LEGALITY:	OBSCENITY								
	CHILDREN								
	ANIMALS								
	BLASPHEMY								
FILM AS A WHOLE				✔					

Comments

Despite appearances this is not really a biker film at all. It fits in less with the Wild Angels cycle [*sic*] than with the James Dean inter-generational pictures. 'My Dad hit harder than that' says Johnny to the men beating him up, and Brando throughout is at his most Dean-like, even reduced to tears at one point. The film is full of adult lectures to the naughty kids who are just 'looking for someone to push them around so they can get sore and show how tough they are'. The *Rebel Without A Cause* theme is emphasised by Johnny's reply to the man who asks what they are rebelling against: 'What have you got?' This is a typical 50s film in that these are not just crazy tearaways but essentially kids let down by their parents (Dad beats Johnny, the girl's uncle is the eager beer seller, her father the cop who ducks his responsibilities). Where 30s films blamed poverty, the 50s blamed the social and psychological poverty of small town and urban life.

The film is also, of course, about 'alien' beings who turn nasty when wet. The townspeople bring the trouble on themselves by putting 'business before pleasure' and supplying endless beers to the gangs (the bar scene here was a conscious inspiration for the scene in *Gremlins*). All the trouble is caused as much by the townspeople as by the bikers with Johnny almost as the Gizmo figure, certainly as much misunderstood as anti-social. The girl sums him up when she notes that he is afraid of her and not vice-versa and draws the parallel between him and her father – both are fakes.

So, the only aspect of the theme that worries me is the glamorisation of alcohol and the continual boozing and drunkenness. As with drugs it is not necessarily enough to point out that the film shows the dangers of alcohol abuse – it may still look attractive and is clearly dangerous when in a drinking and driving context. The film never takes an uncritical view of the bikers or presents them as heroic. Nor are they likely role models for kids today. They are too old and the film is so firmly set in 50s America.

Visually there is little to challenge 'PG' with the terrorisation of the girl (from 47.20) and the beating of Johnny (1.00.05) the strongest moments. The rioting never gets seriously under way and most of the violence we see is perpetrated by the townsmen. There is nothing remotely like the pitched battle of Coppola's teen gang film *The Outsiders*.

Which leaves only the political aspect. Should a long-banned, later X certificate film, only seen on TV late at night, be PG? In my opinion time has drawn the supposed sting from the film, but there will be those who will disagree – without bothering to see the film itself at all. To satisfy this point of view it is doubtful if even a 15 would make much sense, for if we accept that the film is 'dangerous' it is presumably most dangerous to adolescents. We are thus forced to choose between 18 and PG if logic is to be our guide. Rationally it should be PG for a film that is both conservative and moral in most respects. On the other hand, one could question the sense of making a decision that is bound to provoke controversy when the film must have minimal interest to anyone under 18 anyway. It is finally a political decision.

(Examiner's Report, 1986)

consideration of the BBFC's published reasons for rejecting sixteen of the 3,438 videos submitted to it in 1987 indicates that classroom work on *The Wild One* can be seen as a way of discussing current issues without having to deal with texts which remain controversial. In August 1987, for example, a series of tragic and senseless killings took place in Hungerford, in Berkshire, the random nature of which horrified consumers of the news on television, radio and in newspapers. There were fears of a new type of social problem, that of emotionally disturbed people killing innocent bystanders at random with firearms, a dreadful occurrence which was more familiar in the United States than in Britain. The BBFC stated in its Annual Report for that year that claims in the popular press to the effect that video viewing contributed to this particular killer's state of mind were irresponsible, but nevertheless felt that 'its duty was to come down on the side of caution'. James Ferman described the contents of some of the videos rejected in that year as follows:

> Although the violence of many of these rejected videos was the work of a lone psychopath, four were concerned with the anti-social violence of gangs. In one, it was a gang of schoolboys led by a psychopathic sadist, in another it was an urban gang seeking to take over a tenement building in the depressed ghetto area of an American city. A third concerned a gang of bikers whose violence was directed exclusively at women, while a fourth featured a gang of survival cultists seeking to inflict violence for its own sake as a rehearsal for political insurrection … another of the rejected videos had a key scene in which the psychotic central character wanders into a suburban street and opens fire at random bystanders. The similarities with Hungerford made this scene unacceptable in every way for a work which, like the other rejects, had no pretensions whatever to serious comment or purpose. (Ferman, BBFC Annual Report, 1987, p. 14.)

It would be wrong to assert that the videos rejected by the BBFC in 1987 are in any direct sense the latterday equivalents of *The Wild One*. Although the texts may have changed, the processes which link real-life social issues, real events, film fictions and the censor's fear of imitation remain. This is clear in the BBFC's current policy on the presentation of glamorous, easily copied weaponry in martial arts films and thrillers aimed at young people. Since the mid-70s the depiction of martial arts weapons known as the 'nunchaka or 'chainsticks' – popularised in the early 70s by Bruce Lee films – has been customarily removed from films. Similarly, after concern by the police, Parliament and in the press in 1987 and 1988 about the noted increase in the number of knife attacks being reported, the BBFC began removing visual emphasis on the use of 'butterfly' knives – a more display-oriented version of the flick knife or switchblade. The connection with the BBFC considerations in the 50s is again marked here: the Nicholas Ray film *Rebel Without a Cause* which, in 1955 starred James Dean as one of the screen's first disturbed teenagers, had a sequence involving a flick-knife fight shortened by the Board. (The video version is the full version of the film.)

Activity 5 Investigating social and historical contexts

Aims

- To allow the students to develop their skills in gathering and assessing material relevant to the contextual study of film texts.
- To promote a clearer understanding of the ways in which social and historical contexts affect an audience's readings of a film text.

Objectives

Students should be able:

- to examine critically the social and historical contexts for the banning of *The Wild One*;
- to stimulate a comparative discussion of their conclusions about these contexts and the contexts for their consumption of film texts in the present.

You will need

The reproduction of the video packaging sleeve for *The Wild One* in Information Sheet 8 (p. 62-3) and the video sleeve for *Terminator 2: Judgment Day* in Information Sheet 9 (p. 64-5).

What you do

Distribute copies of the two video sleeves and ask the students to compare the images used in marketing these films on video. They should look at: how people and places are represented; what the written information tells us; typeface and layout styles; target audience; distributors and producers; genre, etc. Use this classroom discussion to encourage the students to gather material of relevance to the 50s context for *The Wild One*.

Notes

Information Sheets 10 and 11 (pp. 66-7 and 68-9) contain contextual material relating to the immediate context for the film: a retrospective description of the event which inspired the story of the film, and the director's view of the film's perspective on this event. These can be introduced at the teacher's discretion.

Throughout the 80s, there was a return to 50s styles of dress among young people and the decade became fashionable in Hollywood. A significant number of films produced in the 80s were set in that decade and a good deal of advertising used idealised images of the period to sell jeans, pizzas, etc., and even some 50s argot – the word hip, for example, gained renewed currency. More recently, youth fashion appears to have moved on to the 60s, along with a parallel shift in interest in Hollywood (e.g. Oliver Stone's *The Doors*).

Students could be informed about the social-historical context by a discussion of the emergence of the concept of the teenager in the postwar period during a decade of relative prosperity in which young people became an economic force to be targeted as consumers of clothes, music, films, etc. Nearly four decades of social change as well as of commercial and popular culture separate us from *The Wild One,* and a discussion about what has changed and what has remained the same offers a useful framework for examining the fears of the censor. Where in previous decades the film industry both in the United States and Britain had addressed a notionally homogeneous audience, the 50s saw mass commercial culture directed towards its most enthusiastic future constituency, the young. *The Wild One* marks something of a transition – it is a film about youth but with a thirty-year-old hero, it addresses young people in its styles and its depiction of rebelliousness, but it also addresses an older audience telling them it needs to 'get tough' to keep young hooligans in order.

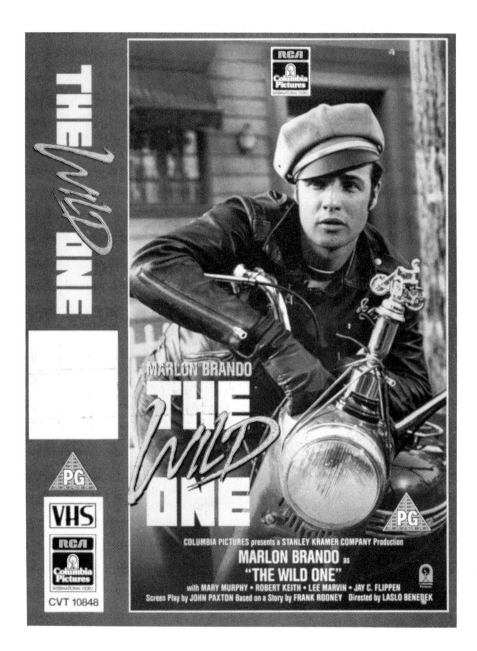

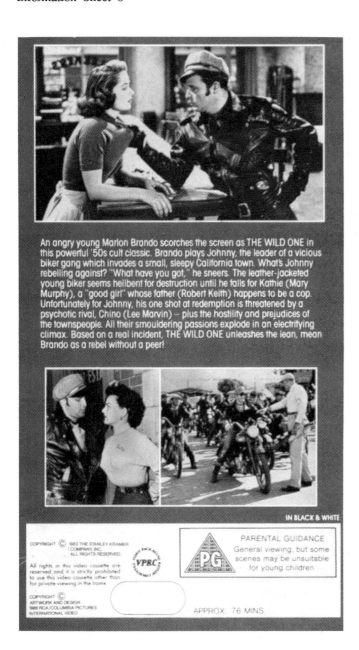

An angry young Marlon Brando scorches the screen as THE WILD ONE in this powerful '50s cult classic. Brando plays Johnny, the leader of a vicious biker gang which invades a small, sleepy California town. What's Johnny rebelling against? "What have you got," he sneers. The leather-jacketed young biker seems hellbent for destruction until he falls for Kathie (Mary Murphy), a "good girl" whose father (Robert Keith) happens to be a cop. Unfortunately for Johnny, his one shot at redemption is threatened by a psychotic rival, Chino (Lee Marvin) — plus the hostility and prejudices of the townspeople. All their smouldering passions explode in an electrifying climax. Based on a real incident, THE WILD ONE unleashes the lean, mean Brando as a rebel without a peer!

IN BLACK & WHITE

VPRC

PARENTAL GUIDANCE
PG
General viewing, but some scenes may be unsuitable for young children

APPROX. 76 MINS.

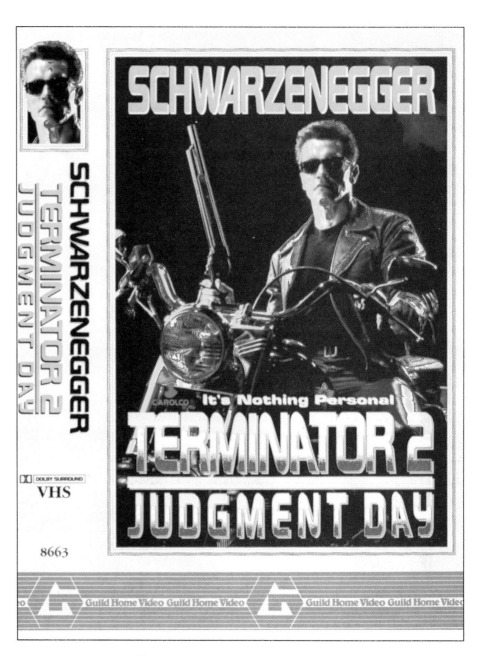

Laslo Benedek review,
Illustrated,
16 April 1955

Why I made

LASLO BENEDEK *tells of America's boy-gang problem and the grim facts*

FOUR thousand young American boys and girls mounted on fast, noisy motor-cycles, invaded the quiet little town of Hollister, in California. In three days of unrestrained chaos, they nearly wrecked Hollister. Speeding back and forth at all hours of the day and night the youths—all members of a motor-cycle club—terrorized the citizens, plundered all the bars and eating houses, reduced the local sheriff to a nervous breakdown and created an upheaval which shocked the whole of America.

That was in July, 1947, and like most people in America, I read about it in my newspaper. It was not the first time such a thing had happened. A few months earlier, a similar gang of teenagers, clad in leather jerkins and blue jeans and wearing goggles and strange club emblems, had appeared in the small town of Riverside, California, with disastrous results.

To me, these incidents were signs of the times, indicating that all was not well with American youth. How did these outbreaks of violence occur? Why had this almost criminal addiction to speed, power and violence taken hold of these young people? I decided to find out. I spent months in research, talked to hundreds of witnesses and practically lived with daredevil members of some of these clubs. The result was a film called *The Wild One*, starring Marlon Brando.

This film is certainly controversial. It is not the usual clear cut hero-and-villain picture with a happy ending. In fact, though it has been shown successfully in the United States and some European countries, it has been banned from most British screens by the refusal of the British Board of Film Censors to give it a certificate—which I am told is a very rare event. Why did I make *The Wild One*? Here are two of the reasons:

First, I believe that a great nation like America can afford to show the more seamy side of its existence.

Secondly, I believe that Hollywood, in so many ways the mirror of America, should stop kidding itself that it can get away much longer with sugary-sweet pictures. It should show life, not only as we would like it, but also as it is. Whatever its demerits, *The Wild One* is realistic. The picture it paints is not a pretty one.

I learnt many things while making this film, but one at least I knew already. As a European who went to America many years ago, I have been shocked by the rôle of violence in American society. People have a strange attitude to it. There is only a superficial moral condemnation of it, and in American films violence is too often the answer to all problems. What Americans call "the Sunday punch" is almost an institution. It is supposed to be the punch that ends the fight. One can say, for instance, that the atom bomb is the Sunday punch of all Sunday punches. But where is it leading us?

America is a young country, and violence is a characteristic of youth, a sign of virility. Among these young kings of the road—the motor-cycle club members—I found violence to be the keynote. Anyone who sees these clubs on the roads at weekends, is frightened, annoyed and puzzled. Sitting centaur-like on their throbbing machines, they can hardly be recognized as individuals. They glory in their "uniform," their anonymity as members of a gang in which all look alike and all think alike.

Don't misunderstand me. Not all motor-cycling clubs are like that. Some are made up of genuine motor enthusiasts. Helped by my friend, the actor Keenan Wynn, who is himself a keen motor-cycle fan, I tried hard to get to know the not-so-good clubs.

Among them I found that accidental violence was the result of too much vitality with too few proper outlets. I found a great deal of irresponsibility; a desire to show off by accomplishing difficult feats; a great satisfaction at being in a gang and obeying whoever proves to be the toughest, the most daring, the most spartan in a curiously cold-blooded manner.

The youngsters I studied were strangely inarticulate. Their language was . . . *engineering*, the language of the machine. They expressed themselves in a series of grunts and groans which they thought very dramatic. I found they craved for freedom from the restrictions and conventions of society. They translated

"The Wild One"

behind the film Britain's censors would not pass

this into the ability to get ahead of traffic, to leave the others standing.

The bulk of them were aged between sixteen and twenty-two (after that they either kill themselves, buy an old jalopy if they can afford it, or settle down).

Mostly they were just out of school. They had small, tedious jobs with little future. Came Saturday or Sunday, and what did the small, quiet, prim American farming town offer them? Or the big, de-personalized city? Nothing but frustration and a feeling of being unwanted.

So we picked Marlon Brando, a magnificent actor whose face expresses a kind of contained power, to play the hero and the villain of the story. We put him at the centre of a chain of events which ends in criminal violence. We tried to show, through him, the uncompromising arrogance of youth, its frustration and its vitality.

We show him secretly craving for recognition and yet fundamentally unable to reveal his feelings because, in his code of conduct, that is a sign of weakness. His attitude to love is typical of many of his contemporaries in real life; to him, love is entirely physical and a close approach to rape. There is no tenderness about it and nothing emotional. These feelings frighten him and he smothers them. He is afraid of falling in love because "To go soft on a girl is weak."

We try also to show the other side of the problem, the reaction of adults to this noisy worshipping of a mechanical god. The film tries to explain the causes of this phenomenon —the lack of interest on the part of older people, the selfish pomposity of age, and fatal encouragement by those who want to gain from the boys' madness.

There are no straight blacks and whites in my story, no simple cases of good and evil, but only realistic middle tones where no one is quite right and no one fully wrong. Life is like that. It would be too simple otherwise.

My angle is a narrow one. It is simply to illustrate incidents which *have* happened as vividly and as truthfully as possible. I present no more than one rough aspect of this strange, dangerous cult of violence and toughness by some youngsters.

It is not my object that everyone should be entertained by *The Wild One*. But reactions so far have shown that all manner of people can *take* this kind of truth and appreciate its meaning.

One last thing. I am a maker of films. To me, a film that is banned from the screen is a negative effort, an undertaking that has come to nought. It is not my place to comment on the ban by the British Board of Film Censors. I can only conclude, with the deepest regret, that somewhere my collaborators and I have not succeeded in convincing those guardians of the British way of life of the sincerity of our purpose.

Extract, Hunter S. Thompson, *Hells Angels*, London 1967, pp. 74-77

The 1947 Hollister hill climb and races also drew contestants from miles around ... many miles, and many contestants. When the sun rose out of the Diablos of the Fourth of July morning the seven-man local police force was nervously sipping coffee after a sleepless night attempting to control something like 3,000 motorcyclists (The police say 4,000; veteran cyclists say 2,000 – so 3,000 is probably about right.) It has been established beyond doubt, however, that Hollister filled up with so many bikes that 1,000 more or less didn't make much difference. The mob grew more and more unmanageable; by dusk the whole downtown area was littered with empty, broken beer bottles, and the cyclists were staging drag races up and down Main Street. Drunken fist fights developed into full scale brawls. Legend has it that the cyclists literally took over the town, defied the police, man-handled local women, looted the taverns and stomped anyone who got in their way. The madness of that week-end got enough headlines to interest an obscure producer named Stanley Kramer and a young actor named Brando. Shortly before her death in 1966, Hollywood gossip columnist Hedda Hopper took note of the Hell's Angels menace and traced its origins back through the years to The Wild One. This led her to blame the whole outlaw phenomenon on Kramer, Brando and everyone else in any way connected with the movie. The truth is that The Wild One – despite an admittedly fictional treatment – was an inspired piece of film journalism. Instead of institutionalizing common knowledge, in the style of Time, it told a story that was only beginning to happen and which was inevitably influenced by the film. It gave the outlaws a lasting romance-glazed image of themselves, a coherent reflection that only a few had been able to find in a mirror, and it quickly became the bike rider's answer to The Sun also Rises. The image is not valid, but its wide acceptance can hardly be blamed on the movie. The Wild One was careful to distinguish between 'good outlaws' and 'bad outlaws', but the people who were most influenced chose to identify with Brando instead of Lee Marvin, whose role as the villain was a lot more true to life than Brando's portrayal of the confused hero. They saw themselves as modern Robin Hoods ... virile, inarticulate brutes whose good instincts got warped somewhere in the struggle for self-expression and who spent the rest of their violent lives seeking revenge on a world that done them wrong when they were young and defenceless.

Another of Hollywood's contributions to the Hell's Angels lore is the name. The Angels say they are named after a famous First World War bomber squadron that was stationed near Los Angeles and whose personnel raced around the area on motorcycles when they weren't airborne. There are others who say the Angels got their name from a 1930 Jean Harlow movie based on some scriptwriter's idea of an Army Air Corps that may or may not have existed at the time of the First World War. It was called Hell's Angels and no doubt was still being shown in 1950, when the restless veterans who founded the first Angels chapter at Fontana were still trying to decide what to do with themselves. While the name might have originated before any Hell's Angel was born, it was lost in the history of some obscure California military base until Hollywood made it famous and also created the image of wild men on motorcycles – an image that was later adopted and drastically modified by a new breed of outcasts that not even Hollywood could conceive of until they appeared, in the flesh, on Californian highways.

The concept of the 'motorcycle outlaw' was as uniquely American as Jazz. Nothing like them had ever existed. In some ways they appeared to be a kind of half breed anachronism, a human hangover from the era of the Wild West. Yet in other ways they were as new as television. There was absolutely no precedent, in the years after the Second World War, for large gangs of hoodlums on motorcycles, revelling in violence, worshipping mobility and thinking nothing of riding five hundred miles on a weekend ... to whoop it up with other gangs of cyclists in some country hamlet entirely unprepared to handle even a dozen peaceful tourists. Many picturesque outback villages got their first taste of tourism not from families driving Fords or Chevrolets, but from clusters of boozing 'city boys' on motorcycles.

In retrospect, eye-witness accounts of the Hollister riot seem timid compared with the film. A more accurate comment on the nature of the Hollister riot is the fact that a hastily assembled force of only twenty-nine cops had the whole show under control by noon of 5 July. By nightfall the main body of cyclists had roared out of town, in the best Time style, to seek new nadirs in sordid behaviour. Those who stayed behind did so at the request of the police; their punishment ranged from $25 traffic fines to ninety days in jail for indecent exposure. Of the 6,000 to 8,000 people supposedly involved in the fracas, a total of fifty were treated for injuries at the local hospital. (For a better perspective on motorcycle riots it helps to keep in mind that more than 450,000 Americans die each year as the result of automobile accidents.)

Nobody has ever accused the Hell's Angels of wanton killing, at least not in court ... but it boggles the nerves to consider what might happen if the outlaws were ever deemed legally responsible for even three or four human deaths, by accident or otherwise. Probably every motorcycle rider in California would be jerked off the streets and ground into hamburger.

For a lot of reasons that are often contradictory, the sight and sound of a man on a motorcycle has an unpleasant effect on the vast majority of Americans who drive cars. At one point in the wake of the Hell's Angels uproar a reporter for the *New York Herald Tribune* did a long article on the motorcycle scene and decided in the course of his research that 'there is something about the sight of a passing motorcyclist that tempts many automobile drivers to commit murder'.

Nearly everyone who has ridden a bike for any length of time will agree. The highways are crowded with people who drive as if their sole purpose getting behind the wheel is to avenge every wrong ever done them by man, beast or fate. The only thing that keeps them in line is their own fear of death, jail and lawsuits ... which are much less likely if they can find a motorcycle to challenge instead of another two-thousand-pound car or a concrete abutment. A motorcyclist has to drive on the road as if everybody else on the road is out to kill him. A few of them are, and many of those who aren't are just as dangerous – because the only thing that can alter their careless, ingrained driving habits is the threat of punishment, either legal or physical, and there is nothing about a motorcycle to threaten any man in a car. A bike is totally vulnerable; its only defence is manoeuverability, and every accident situation is potentially fatal – especially on a freeway, where there is no room to fall without being run over almost instantly. Despite these hazards, California – where freeways are a way of life – is by long odds the nation's biggest motorcycle market

Reproduced by permission of Penguin Books Ltd.

Activity 6 Textual analysis

Aim

• To develop the students' skills in textual analysis in relation to a media text.

Objective

• Students should be able to consider different ways of viewing a film extract and to increase understanding of the various ways in which texts address audiences.

You will need
Video clip 3: *The Wild One* and Activity Sheet 4 (p. 71).

The extract is $9\frac{1}{2}$ min. long and is taken from 17 min. into the film after the Black Rebels have arrived in the small town. It may be broken down into five sequences for discussion purposes:

1. The Bikers in the Street: They kill time by playing on pogo sticks, riding around beer bottles on their motorcycles. Doc directs them towards the bar for more beer and tells them about the hotel.
2. The Street: A connecting sequence. Two young women from the town make their way to the bar past the bikers loitering outside. The men follow them inside.
3. The Bar: Jimmy, the elderly barman employed by Doc, serves the young men and the two women. The Coffee Bar: Johnny and Kathie talk to each other about their different experiences.
4. The Bar: The bikers play music and instruct Jimmy in their 'jive' talk and 'bebop' music. The bikers dance with the two women to music on the jukebox.
5. The Coffee Bar: Johnny instructs two of the gang to drink the coffee they have ordered. Johnny's conversation with

Kathie is interrupted by her policeman father. Johnny ignores the policeman's attempts to talk to him and leaves the bar.

What you do
The sequences contained within the extract concern the meeting of various groups and ideas to produce a dramatic effect. The students should be asked to make explicit the contrasting pairs of elements before discussing how, in their view, these elements could have contributed to the censor's reactions to *The Wild One*. A list of such contrasting categories would include:

Youth	–	Age
Kathie, Johnny, bikers	–	Jimmy, Doc,
Young women from town		policeman
Strangers	–	Townspeople
Johnny, bikers	–	Jimmy, young
		women,
		Doc, Kathie,
		policeman
Protagonists	–	Background
		figures
Johnny, Kathie, Jimmy	–	Harmonica-
		playing biker,
Policeman	–	Coffee-drinking
		bikers

By analysing the sequence in some detail, it should be possible to direct classroom discussion towards the interrelationship of these elements and back towards the censor's belief in the 50s that *The Wild One* was such a potentially dangerous film to show young people that it had to be banned for adults as well. For example, sequences 3 and 5 in the extract overtly depict the meeting of youth and age in terms of values: Jimmy expresses his dislike of excitement (television, radio news, 'pictures and noise' – i.e. the very basis of cinema); while the young men express the

Activity Sheet 4

Questions on the video extract from *The Wild One*

1. Write a brief account of what Jimmy, the old barman, told his wife when he got home the evening after serving the motorcyclists in the bar. Alternatively, draw the events as seen from his point of view in a storyboard.

2. List the elements in the extract which refer to youth styles. Do you think some things have changed? Have any of the things you have listed stayed the same?

3. What do you think we are meant to feel about:

   • Johnny?
   • Kathie?
   • The bikers in the bar?
   • Jimmy?
   • The bar owner, Doc?

values of their group through their use of 'jive' talk, a 50s argot associated with the 'white hipster' who based his view of the world on the real-life 'black rebels' of modern jazz in the 40s, whose music it is that the young man plays on the harmonica and performs in the form of 'bop' vocals (a form of music which the students may recognise as an antecedent to rap music).

Examine the extract closely with the students and direct them towards questioning how they would set about discovering the film's perspective on its subject matter. What do they believe they are being encouraged to think about the various characters? The questions on Activity Sheet 4 (p. 71) could be of use in focusing discussion.

Activity 7 Representation

Aim

- To engage the students with the way in which film texts deal with society and groups within society.

Objectives

Students should be able:

- to discuss how representations of young people in the media have changed, or not, since *The Wild One*;
- to assess critically how or whether media representations of groups in society should be regulated.

You will need

Activity Sheet 5 (p. 73), 'Editorial, *Motorcycling*'. You may also find Information Sheets 10 and 11 (pp. 66-67 and 68-9) useful for this work as they provide arguments for *The Wild One* having been seen as a realistic depiction of a social problem in the 50s, whereas it is probable that the students will now view it as a genre piece.

What you do

Distribute Activity Sheet 5 (p. 73), which contains a question involving a simulation. The students could be split into groups each forming an editorial committee to compose a piece replying to the concerns expressed by the editorial writers of *Motorcycling*.

Notes

The piece from *Motorcycling* supports the ban on *The Wild One* because it feels the reputation of its readership is tarnished by the representation of motorcyclists in the film. This is a relatively unimportant example of a serious issue in the consideration of the relationship between the media and society. Central to this consideration are representations

Motor Cycling
27 January 1955

PROPRIETORS :
TEMPLE PRESS LIMITED

CHAIRMAN AND MANAGING DIRECTOR :
ROLAND E. DANGERFIELD

Head Office : BOWLING GREEN LANE, LONDON, E.C.1
Telephone : Terminus 3636. *Telegrams :* "Pressimus, Phone, London."
Birmingham—7 John Bright Street.   *Telephone :* Midland 4117-8
Coventry—50 Hertford Street.   *Telephone :* Coventry 62464
Manchester—1 Brazennose Street.   *Telephone :* Blackfriars 5038-9.
Glasgow—12 Renfield Street.   *Telephone :* Glasgow Central 1413

READ WHEREVER MOTORCYCLES ARE RIDDEN

Editor : R. R. HOLLIDAY

Consulting Editor : GRAHAM WALKER

Vol. XCI. No. 2348   January 27, 1955   Annual Subscription Rate : 44s.
(U.S.A. and Canada : $7.00)

EDITORIAL

We Want No "Wild Ones" Here

WHEN a film company produces a major film starring so renowned an actor as Marlon Brando, and the British Board of Film Censors withholds a certificate for its exhibition, that is general news. When it is learned that the plot of the film is based entirely on the anti-social activities of a gang of American toughs calling themselves the Black Rebels Motorcycle Club, then the matter clearly calls for comment on this page.

The film is entitled "The Wild One," and, having seen a synopsis of its story, we can quite understand why the production has not received the censor's approval.

"Violence," begins the synopsis, "hovers like a cloud over the little town from the minute the Black Rebels Motorcycle Club blows in." An outlaw gang, the "club," which uses well-known British and American machines, has just been ordered away from a legitimate motorcycle meeting and is "spoiling for trouble."

"After that," we read, "you could have a hundred heads and not see all that happens. Kid riders burning up the streets. Others riding in and out of the bar. More drag races. Riders insulting people for no very good reason except that they feel like insulting people."

With complete candour, the synopsis continues to describe further acts of lawlessness in which children are all but run down, a beauty salon is wrecked and eventually an old man is killed by the "hero's" runaway machine. A stern sheriff at last orders ringleader Johnny (Mr. Brando) out of the district and, we are finally told, "Johnny nearly hits a dog as his machine roars out of town after the rest of the Black Rebels, who have gone on ahead. He swerves, swears, stops, kicks his starter again, rides on. Johnny's thoughts are his own. He has been helped out of some real trouble by some people who had no real cause to help him. If it has changed him, we can't tell—not surely, anyway—as he roars around a bend

and out of sight of the town he had helped to paralyse with fear for a day and a night."

That such goings-on do occur in America we are well aware. But that they should be considered fit material for an important film is something we cannot understand, particularly as this picture does not even appear to attempt to point a moral. Nor can we believe that the best way to persuade the world's youth to respect law and order is to put entirely contrary ideas into its head. There are many splendid facets of the American way of life which other nations appreciate and attempt to emulate: there are also some bad ones, among them being the hooligan gangs that do so much to harm the reputation of organized motorcycling. To their great credit, British riders have scorned these playboy antics and we want nothing in this country that could possibly have any detrimental influence on the more ebullient young members of our fraternity.

Losing on the Swings— and the Roundabouts !

EVERYWHERE it is agreed that it the nation is prospering, then it is time that prices came down—and the country looks to private enterprise to give consumers some benefit from profits, and to the Government to relax taxation, particularly on Income, Purchase and Petrol taxes, which are the three that directly affect practically all citizens.

But what happens? Private enterprise puts up the price of all grades of petrol, meaning that all goods and services dependent on motor spirit will cost more. And, just as we were about to remark that the inevitable increase in transport fares might mean more interest in motorcycles, especially the highly economical "clip-on"—bingo, Mr. Butler clamps a 25% P.T. levy on it!

In the phrase of the Black Country, "We'm beggered all roads! "

FOOTNOTE: Although written before the Chancellor's announcement, "Carbon's" note this week on "clip-ons" is now even more pertinent.

B5

The editor appears to support the censor's decision to ban *The Wild One* because the film would reflect badly on his readers. Imagine that you are a reader of *Motorcycle* magazine but also the editor of the following (imaginary) magazine:

Waddayagot? The Official British Marlon Brando fanzine.

- What would you write in your editorial for February 1955? How would you crop the image from the poster for your magazine's article?

A recent poster advertisement stressing the 'freedom' offered by purchasing a Kawasaki motorcycle also contained verbal advice to cyclists to act responsibly to maintain the image of motorcyclists in general.

- Can you think of any other circumstances in which advertisers may feel it necessary to add advice like this?

- What purpose do you think it serves?

of race and gender. Classroom discussion of this topic could broaden out into the difficult question of whether regulation of racist, homophobic or misogynistic representations in films is to be subject to law. The isolation of the not so pressing issue of the representation of motorcyclists here, allows the students to think about the various sources from which calls for censorship or regulation can emerge. When the comedy film A *Fish Called Wanda* (UK, Charles Crichton, 1988) was transmitted on network television in December 1991, for example, some of the stuttering of one central character was removed to limit the possible offence to viewers with a speech defect. American television practically eliminated this character in a bid to remove the possibility of offence. The release in Japan of the comedy thriller *Men at Work* (US, Emilio Estevez, 1990) about two young dustmen who discover a corpse amongst the refuse was met with calls for censorship from the Japanese refuse collector's union, who felt that the film was suggesting that men who did this vital work should be seen as second-class citizens.

It is clear that narrative contexts and genre are important factors in assessing likely offence. Can the students think of contexts in which specific representations of groups in society would offer justifiable cause for censorship? You might find it useful as part of this exercise to consider more recent representations aimed at young people – the Madonna material in section 4, for example.

Activity 8 Describing a film and the circulation of secondary texts: publicity, reviews, synopses

Introduction
It should be apparent to the students that the way films are described and the context in which ideas about them are read has a great effect on the way audiences perceive them. Descriptions of films can predispose certain audiences to have greater or lesser degrees of anticipation, or even trepidation, when it comes to horror films for example, about the kind of emotions and pleasures they are going to experience. Later in this workbook, there will be an opportunity for students to examine the various ways in which critics discuss films and how this may relate to audience demands for regulation (see section 8). Here, various descriptions and synopses of the film can be compared, from the descriptions of *The Wild One* by the censor in the 50s, quoted earlier, to the promotional blurb on the videocassette packaging in 1992. This is quite a difficult exercise but a productive one. Descriptions by critics and publicists, as well as censors and young people, can focus on certain parts of the film and not others. Pupils should be encouraged to consider why it is that it is impossible to fully describe the experience of watching a film in words.

Aim

- To develop an increased understanding of the circulation process and role played by secondary sources of information about film texts.

Objective

- Students should be able to distinguish between description and comment in verbal descriptions of film and video texts.

You will need

Activity Sheet 6 (p. 78) and copies of the three synopses of the film on Information Sheets 8, 12 and 13 (pp. 62-3, 76 and 77). The synopsis on sheet 8 is part of the overall design of a video sleeve. Sheet 12 is an unsuccessful attempt at a relatively value-free synopsis, while the description on sheet 13 is potentially the most productive. It is an attempt by a newspaper to offer a short story based on the narrative of the film after it was banned, as a way of answering the question: 'Was the censor right to ban *The Wild One?*'

What you do

Distribute the synopses and Activity Sheet 6.

The Wild One, USA, 1953

The members of the Black Rebels motor-cycle club, riding in menacing near-military formation, bear down on a country motor-cycle race meeting. They loiter about the track, getting in the way of the racers; and before they are finally moved on by the police, one of the gang steals a statuette from among the prizes and presents it to Johnny, their leader. They move into a peaceful little town, where, in a scrimmage in the main square, one of them is slightly injured when he runs his motor-cycle into a car driven by an elderly man. While waiting in the local bar for his return from hospital, Johnny gets into conversation with Kathie, a young waitress. A rival gang arrives, and Chino, its leader, provokes Johnny to a fight, a sort of ritual demonstration of strength. The fight spreads when a townsman tries to intervene, and Chino is taken off to gaol. Towards evening an ugly situation develops; the hooligans embark on a course of casual, unmotivated destruction; the police officer, Kathie's father, lacks the strength of will to intervene, and a group of townspeople decide to take the law into their own hands. Rescuing Kathie from some of his own followers, Johnny rides away with her; but she is frightened, and unsure of her own feelings for him, and runs away. Assuming that Johnny has attempted to assault her, the townsfolk capture him and beat him up. Johnny escapes, retrieves his cycle, but is knocked off it: the machine runs on, out of control, and a man is killed. The arrival of the county sheriff restores order, and Johnny is let off with a caution when the sheriff learns from Kathie and her father the facts about the man's death. Before riding away, Johnny returns to the bar; he leaves the stolen statuette with Kathie.

(Monthly Film Bulletin, 1953)

David Lewin review, © Daily Express, 29 January 1955

SATURDAY SPECIAL

FICTION

—story of the banned film

This is the story of the Marlon Brando film "The Wild One," which the British censor has banned. There is no certificate for it—not even an 'A' or an 'X,' because the censor fears the story might affect teen-agers. DAVID LEWIN has seen the film and he has written this story.

Here is the story. Now you decide: Was the censor right to ban "The Wild One"?

Brando as "Johnny"

THE day the motor-cyclists raided, the sun shone down on the long, hard road into the town. It was a town the cyclists had never heard of before. They roared their machines through the avenue of trees into the main street with its cluster of shops, its bar, and its wooden framed houses.

The cyclists came in almost military formation. At the head, wearing a black shiny leather jacket with a remnant of an officer's stars on the shoulder tabs, was their leader, Johnny.

The other cyclists crowded in behind him talking in a special jive language of their own: "Hi, fellas—drag for beers. Who wants to drag for beers? Last guy in the door of the bar buys the beers."

Their names were as crazy as their talk: "Hi, Mouse," "Hi, Go-Go," "Hi, Gringo"—"Hi, Crazy." Their machines they called "sickles." They called themselves "The Black Rebels.

They had just been run out of one town for interfering with a regular meeting of an ordinary motor-cycle club. The policeman there had said: "Get going, you guys. I've seen enough of you to last me for ever. Now hit the road or I'll put the whole bunch of you away for a month."

THEY looked the policeman between the eyes, and they roared down the hard, dusty road the policeman said: "They're just looking for someone to run them around so they can get sore and show how tough they are."

In the small, quiet town they

came to they crowded into the bar dragging for beers. Their leader, Johnny, swung a statuette which he had picked up from the motor-cycle rally they had left. It was gold coloured and it did not belong to him. He had just "organised it."

☆

IN the café a young girl was serving coffee. Johnny looked at her and thrust the statuette in front of her. "You can have it," he said.

The girl, Kathie looked at him: "But you can't do that. You can't give away something you won to a girl unless you know her really well and you like her."

Johnny spooned his coffee, and the girl looked at him and asked: "Where are you going to when you leave here?"

Johnny said: "You just go. You don't go any one special place. You just go. A bunch gets together after working all week, and it builds up and you just go."

Outside the bar there was

a roaring from motor-cycle engines. A rival gang to the Black Rebels had come into town. Their leader was a tall, bearded youngster with a striped shirt. He called himself Chino. He rushed at Johnny and snatched the gold statuette.

The motor-cyclists crowded out of the bar and formed a circle, tensely waiting. Johnny said: "Put it back, Chino, put it back." And then they fought.

Harry, the local policeman, vainly tried to separate them. A man in a car attempted to get through the mob driving his way home and immediately the motor-cyclists forgot their own fight and attacked the man.

"Over it goes," they chanted, advancing on the car, "we'll turn the car over."

☆

THE policeman seized Chino, and said: "Break 'k up, break it up." There were protests: "But the man in the car tried to run us down." The policeman looked around at their smiling faces. "All right," he said to the man in the car, "I'll take you and this motor-cyclist to the lock-up with me."

The sun was setting now and around the motorcyclists were sitting around on the kerb, staring at their machines and wondering what to do next.

Someone cried: "Let's get Chino out of the jail." In minutes they had broken into the prison and Chino was out.

Harry, the policeman sat in his office, drumming his fingers on the blotting-pad. He picked up the phone and said: "Get me the State Police." Then the line went dead.

The motor-cyclists were at the town telephone exchange wrecking the switchboard.

off in the gloom of the evening to a park outside town.

There he stopped, and they faced one another. The girl said: "I can't fight back. I'm too tired. You'd like me to fight back, then you could hit me."

Johnny said: "You think you're too good for me. Anybody thinks they're too good for me, I knock them over some time."

They stared at one another for a few minutes more in the darkness, and the girl said softly: "I know how you feel. You're always fighting, aren't you? Why do you hate everybody? Sometimes I hate everybody too—I even hate myself. But you can't go on hating."

Almost gently he took her back to the machine, and they rode off to town. He said: "It's over now. We'll be leaving right away."

In town the citizens were gathering and taking the law into their own hands. One of

them had gone for the State Police. The others gathered together with sticks and an odd rifle.

When Johnny rode into town they seized him and hauled him into a corner and there they started beating him.

The town policeman broke up the group. "Leave the boy alone," he ordered. "This is a job for the law."

But Charlie, the man in the car, argued : "We're just pounding a little respect for law into this guy's thick skull."

Blindly, Johnny staggered away from them to his motor-cycle. His face was bruised and through his tears he felt for the handlebars, slung himself on and weaved down the street.

In a daze something hit him on the back of his head. He fell. As he did so the machine swung wildly across . . . an old man was there in front of him . . . being run down.

WHEN the State Troopers came Johnny was back in the police station and the Black Rebels and the other motorcyclists were being rounded up. They charged Johnny with manslaughter.

Then strangely two of the townsmen stuffed forward and said: "It wasn't really his fault. Someone threw him from his bar and hit him as he was driving and he didn't know."

The sheriff looked at Johnny: "I'm going to take a big fat chance with you. I'm going to release you. You'll face another charge later but it won't be manslaughter."

Johnny, his head down, slunk out of the police station. "Aren't you going to say thank you?" said the sheriff. Kathie, the girl said softly: "It's all right—he doesn't know how."

IT was almost dawn as the motor-cyclists drove down that long, hard road from the town. They looked like a collection of animals that had been left out in the rain all night.

Johnny went back to the bar and saw the girl there, and said not a word. But on the counter he left the golden statuette. Then he drove fast down the street from the bar. And as he went the sunlight was just filtering through the trees over the dusty road.

THEY saw Kathie coming out of the bar and surrounded her, driving their motor-cycles round and round in a decreasing circle. Johnny saw her and raced in. They let him through.

Johnny saw him scoop up the terrified girl, put her on the back of his machine and roar

1. Study the documents:

   - Information Sheet 8 (p. 62-3): Video packaging sleeve for *The Wild One*.
   - Information Sheet 13 (p. 77): 'Saturday Fiction Special – story of the banned film' – *Daily Express*, 29 January 1955.
   - Information Sheet 12 (p. 76): Synopsis – *Monthly Film Bulletin*, June 1953.

Each of the synopses attempts at different lengths to tell the story of the film *The Wild One*. Each of them contains the following:

   - a description of the main events;
   - an introduction of the main characters and an indication of their motivations in the story.

Each of the synopses also suggests what kind of emotions and pleasures watching *The Wild One* will give the audience. Which synopsis tells us most about the following:

   - the narrative?
   - Johnny?
   - Kathie?
   - Chino?

2. Which of the synopses would most make you want to see this film? Why?

3. Each synopsis comes from a very different type of publication. Does each synopsis expect a different kind of reader? Discuss the possible functions that each synopsis could serve.

4. Rewrite the synopsis for one of these magazines:

   - A music teenage magazine (e.g. *Smash Hits*);
   - a video release summary; a programme, schedule listing. (100 words)
   - *Radio Times*: a film preview. (50 words)
   - Press release from satellite television company (e.g. a movie channel) to regional papers advertising screening at 10.00 p.m. on Saturday. (150 words)

3   The regulation of depictions of violence: *Platoon* (US, Oliver Stone, 1986)

Introduction

This section deals with a more recent film representing violence in war and, arguably, addressing young people. It is intended to use Oliver Stone's 1986 Vietnam war film *Platoon* to focus class discussion on the regulation and classification of violent imagery – the considerations which have been brought to bear on this by regulators and the views and ideas of the pupils based on their own viewing experiences and choices. The suggested activities need to be accompanied by a video extract for classroom use at the teacher's discretion. This unit's aims are to introduce these issues by:

* presenting information on how regulatory institutions have attempted to approach representations of violence, either through codes of practice or by reference to social science research;
* using the case of *Platoon* to focus the students' attention on an individual text, so that the ideas introduced can be measured against the evidence of one particular representation of violence in one set of contexts.

Background

Earlier regulation codes

In the forty-three rules governing film censorship in the 20s there were only five which dealt with images of violence. This is surprising, perhaps, in the light of the perennial concerns expressed about violence in the media. The five rules in question disallowed:

1. Cruelty to young infants and excessive cruelty and torture to adults, especially women.
2. The exhibition of profuse bleeding.
3. Gruesome murders and strangulation scenes.
4. Executions.
5. The effect of vitriol throwing.

The last two are extremely specific and the worry about executions probably had a political component – a concern that graphic depictions of hangings could turn people against the then public policy of capital punishment. In the 90s, although the BBFC, as has been previously mentioned, does not have a code of this sort, its practice on images of violence bears a distant affinity with these rules. For example, details of hanging are generally removed from films in the lower categories in case they provoke imitation. Vitriol throwing refers to a criminal technique, representation of which worried the BBFC in the 20s. In the 80s potentially instructional techniques of lock-picking, car stealing and, in connection with violence, violent manoeuvres such as 'double ear claps' – blows to the eardrums with the cupped palms of the hand – neck breaks and emphatic blows to the crotch are occasionally removed from martial arts films in all categories on a similar basis. A major difference between the application of these codes then and of institutional regulatory practice on violent images now, is that in the 20s this concern took a back seat to the more openly political agenda of the other thirty-eight rules, so that *Battleship Potemkin* was banned as a Bolshevik film, but also as a Bolshevik film with violent sequences (i.e. the legendary Odessa Steps sequence).

During the 30s, the decade in which Hollywood studios elevated the gangster to the status of a major screen genre figure, Hollywood films began to be governed by The Motion Picture Production Code. The Code was a self censorship device instigated by the studios in order to fend off the threat of the kind of pre-censorship of films conducted by the BBFC and other European boards. Instituted in 1930, it emerged from the office of Will H. Hays (and is often referred to as The Hays Code), a Republican politician who was hired by the film industry to prevent public scandals involving stars (such as the Fatty Arbuckle affair in which a party at the comedian's house had led to the death of a starlet) and persuade the producers of films to avoid upsetting moral campaigners with controversial films. It became effective, however, only when it adopted strategies of economic coercion by issuing 'seals of approval' without which major distributors would not distribute the film (see also the discussion of self-regulation in section 8). Of the twelve listed applications of the Code the second was entitled 'Brutality' and states: 'Excessive and inhuman acts of cruelty and brutality shall not be presented. This includes all detailed and protracted presentation of physical violence, torture and abuse.' Another subsection under application one, 'Crime', concerned murder and stated, among other things, that 'brutal killings should not be presented in detail'.

The most striking aspect of O'Connor's rules governing representations of violence and the relevant sections of the Hollywood Production Code of the 30s is that they concentrate mostly on what is presented rather than *how it is* presented. Although the Production Code section on 'Crime' had a section stipulating that the sympathies of the audience should not be directed towards the criminal, how this proscribed perspective is likely to be created by the film is left unquestioned: the Hays office would recognise it when it saw it. (In fact, the gangster films of the 30s, like many excellent subsequent entries in their genre, such as Martin Scorsese's *Goodfellas* (US, 1990) and Barry Levinson's *Bugsy* (US, 1992), created sympathy for and fascination with their criminal protagonists.)

As with most earlier attempts to legislate in this area through guidelines for producers, juries and censors to follow, the question of how regulations attempt to distinguish between different representations of the same narrative event is a central one and codes have relied on such phrases as 'in detail' and 'detailed and protracted', leaving it open to wide interpretation to which depictions this could apply. As acts of violence occur in the narrative of many films, videos and television programmes, the question of how something is portrayed is very important.

'Video violence' in the 80s – attempts at guidelines

During the early 80s, the public controversy concerning 'video violence' led to numerous erratic applications of the Obscene Publications Act (OPA) by different police forces up and down the country who were clearly facing an issue which, as classroom discussion should serve to illustrate, is not one for which easy conclusions are available. This situation prompted the then Director of Public Prosecutions to frame a set of written guidelines for deciding whether videos containing sequences of violence, which usually turned out to be horror videos, should be proceeded against under the obscenity legislation. Information Sheet 14 (p. 81) contains a quotation from the Attorney General's written statement to Parliament in July 1984 concerning representations of violence in videos and the OPA. It stresses as does the OPA, that each video has to be seen as a whole – that narrative and other contexts are likely to be important – and extends the definition of 'obscenity', which has traditionally only described sexual imagery, to address the concerns of those groups and their representatives in Parliament who had made the issue of violent representations in video a matter for legal consideration. It also then attempts to face up to the problem that depictions of violence are, unlike sex scenes in films setting out to titillate, invariably embedded in a narrative which gives the scenes themselves various meanings. It is possible to imagine a film which is a collection of sequences depicting violence, without the audience being given any perspective on who the screen figures were or why the depicted violence was occurring. It may be productive to discuss this scenario with the students. Assuming, as the law and the censor does, that people can be corrupted by watching films or videos, would a video containing sequences of staged violence and nothing else – no characters, no motivations, no plot – be a corrupting one, that is to say, in the censor and the law's definition, obscenely violent? Or would the audience be looking for clues to the meaning of the scenes – by looking at the dress of the characters, the locations in which the scenes are taking place,

Statement by Attorney General, July 1984:

The basic factor is that the test of obscenity is the tendency to deprave and corrupt those who are, having regard to all the circumstances, likely to see it. The DPP therefore has to consider who is likely to view videos taken into the home. While this is ultimately for the court to decide in each particular case, the DPP considers that, in many cases, a significant number of the viewers will be children or young people. In applying this basic factor, the film is considered as a whole. But each episode has to be examined on its own before being considered as part of the film as a whole.

The following questions may be relevant:

1. Who is the perpetrator of the violence, and what is his reaction to it?
2. Who is the victim, and what is his reaction?
3. How is the violence inflicted, and in what circumstances?
4. How explicit is the description of the wounds, mutilation or death? How prolonged? How realistic?
5. Is the violence justifiable in narrative terms?

A work is likely to be regarded as obscene if it portrays violence to such a degree and so explicitly that its appeal can only be to those who are disposed to derive positive enjoyment from seeing such violence.

Other factors may include:

• violence perpetrated by children;
• self-mutilation;
• violent abuse of women or children;
• cannibalism;
• use of vicious weapons (e.g. broken bottle);
• use of everyday implements (e.g. screwdriver, shears, electric drill);
• violence in a sexual context.

These factors are not exhaustive. Style can also be important. The more convincing the depictions of violence, the more harmful it is likely to be. But, in any event, these factors cannot be conclusive of the Director's decision in a particular case. He also has to have regard to the standards set by the courts – hence the arrangements for the results of concluded cases to be passed to the Board.

the camera angles with which it is shot, etc. – in order to provide their own context? In one sense, such a video or film would offer a 'worse case' scenario for a regulatory body because it would offer no narrative justification whatever for what was being shown. Avoiding the question of 'harm' for the moment, would it also be a video which would cause a good deal of public complaint and disquiet if it were to be distributed widely?

This scenario indicates, of course, that there is nearly always a clear context for violent scenes and the five considerations, listed (1) – (5) in the Attorney General's statement are really an attempt to find a way of answering (5) – 'Is the violence justifiable in narrative terms?' The first two questions indicate that what could be censorable, to return to John Trevelyan's formulation, are certain 'messages' about violence which seem to be implicit in representations of violence which are lengthy and 'realistic' and in certain contexts. A sequence which seemed to be saying that 'it is fun to beat up helpless victims' and, while not contradicting that message in the narrative context, demonstrated the 'fun' with a good deal of detail should clearly be more censorable than, let us say, an action hero like Jean Claude van Damme elegantly polishing off baddies in balletic martial arts sequences.

Activity 9 Narrative, genre and depictions of violence

Aim

- To investigate the role of narrative and genre in depictions of violence and their regulation.

Objective

- Students should be able to identify a correlation between the depictions of violence, their regulation and their audiences.

What you do

Without inviting them to conjure up their own brutal scenarios, ask the students to consider possible pairs of perpetrators/victims and imagine whether a screen depiction of aggression involving them would be more or less likely to cause:

- upset to them as individual viewers;
- distress to other viewers or complaint by the public;
- the regulators to believe a sequence could be 'harmful' in the sense implied by the Attorney General's statement.

Examples of Perpetrator/Victim

Policeman	Criminal
Mugger	Person in street
Alien monster	Spaceship crew member
Sheriff	Outlaw
Teenage gang member	Rival gang member
Kung fu expert, hero	Kung fu expert, villain
Kung fu expert	Unskilled opponent
Husband	Wife
Serial killer etc.	Randomly chosen victim

Ask the students to invent or gather together a list of such pairs and discuss the following questions:

1. What if the perpetrator/victim roles were reversed in the scene?
2. Are there different dramatic circumstances in which the depicted violence would be more or less upsetting for them as viewers? Take as an example:

   (a) policeman shoots criminal as he holds hostages at gunpoint;
   (b) policeman beats up suspected criminal in a cell.

3. How does gender fit into the above list? The class could try attaching genders to each of the fictional character-types listed and discuss the results.

Notes

With the above list of fictional screen perpetrators and victims of violence, it is apparent that not only are wider narrative considerations suggested by the mere choice of protagonists, but that a type of film is also unavoidably implied. This is also likely to be the case with the students' own list. Does the idea of genre make a difference, then, to the way the Attorney General's list of considerations conceptualises screen violence? This statement was produced in response to concern in the press and among sections of the public about violence in films on video, and this concern tended to focus on films which could be described as horror films. The reference to an 'alien monster' and a 'serial killer' in the list of screen perpetrators and victims suggest this genre and horror films, by virtue of their intention of horrifying audiences are more likely to represent violence in details than some other genres. Horror films, even good horror films, are also less likely to have much in the way of character motivation to contextualise the violence than other genres, being more interested in the audience's fear than its understanding. This is one reason why, despite its long, and occasionally distinguished history, the horror genre has been traditionally disapproved of by the censor, some critics and members of the public. Conversely, certain genres, such as the Western, conventionally feature violent representations which are less likely to concern regulatory bodies and upset audiences.

'Video violence' regulation

The BBFC, in taking responsibility for the classification of videos, has to address the question of depictions of violence in videos as a central aspect of its work. In 1985, the BBFC published a short 'Guide to Obscenity Law and Video Violence' as part of its Annual Report in that year. This took the DPP's guidelines as a starting point and added that the most important aspect of seeing representations of violence in the framework of 'obscenity' is 'immoral influence'. For James Ferman, the guide's author, 'immoral influence' would be discerned in the intentions of the film-maker, whose sympathies could be read from the film by the BBFC and the reference to the Williams Committee's definition of the dangerously violent video which leads into the consideration of immoral influence is close to the scenario of the imaginary video discussed earlier. This statement by the censor indicates that not only is the explicitness of the depiction of violence – the 'degree of detail' referred to by the old Hollywood Production Code – the only issue to be measured against the context of narrative and genre, but that the perspective of the film-maker – seen as identical to the 'values' of the film – is also important.

For Ferman, as for the DPP and the Williams Committee, individual violent films – particularly films featuring violence towards women in a sexual context – can be considered obscene. Ferman in creating BBFC's daily procedure on violence, however, adds that it is not just one film that provides the context for individual sequences of violence but a series of similar films offering the same pleasures. This policy is laid out the BBFC's Annual Report of 1988 (Information Sheet 15 (p. 85)). The basis for this is the concept of conditioning. This is a psychological idea describing how the process by which the behaviour of a conscious organism becomes dependent on an event occurring in its environment. An example of a conditional response would be a dog salivating at the sound of a bell because food has always been put before it when the bell has been rung previously. Their model for the way people may respond to representations of violence relies on the idea of images of violence as a respected stimulus which may 'disinhibit' viewers from committing violent acts in the real world, or 'desensitize' them to the consequences of real-life violence. The policy means that representations of violence are cut from video by the BBFC even for the adult '18' category, as well as to achieve lower categories such as '15' and 'PG'. In 1988, the Board cut 63 minutes from fifty-four video features and seven films, with respect to this policy, out of a total of 234 videos requiring cuts and 49 films which were cut. (In all, 2,556 videos and 337 films were submitted to the BBFC in that year.) The policy has its main reference point in psychologically based research such as Donnerstein's and Malamuth's (1984), but it is not explicitly based on it as all research in these areas tends to be inconclusive and strongly contested.

Television

The arguments put by James Ferman about the relationship between depictions of violence and obscenity law call upon regulations to attempt to assess the inherent morality of individual films in the wider context of a series of films. Enid Wistrich (formerly a member of the Greater London Council Film Board) has argued for an end to adult censorship. She engaged with this policy in the context of Stephen Murphy's tenure as the GLCFB's Secretary and claimed that the reason for cutting extreme details in the depiction of violence had less to do with notions of morality than with the limitation of public complaint. What, she conjectured, if it were better, morally, for people to be upset by screen violence rather than accepting it as an entertainment? Was it more of a danger

to make representations of violence more acceptable to audiences by removing details which may not be corrupting, but may serve to upset the audience sufficiently to provoke them to search for more probable crimes of violence in the real world – such social problems, for example, as unemployment, injustice, alcohol abuse, women's status in society – as a first step to doing something about them (Wistrich, 1976, p. 127.) Martin Barker, (1984, p. 104) puts a similar argument. If the censor's view points to one type of audience, does Wistrich's point to another? If Wistrich is right and the desired end result is to limit criticism, is increased criticism of the way films represent violence likely to lead for calls for greater censorship?

With television, the eye of the regulators is sharply focused on the possibility and consequences of audience complaints rather than on 'obscenity'. The broadcasting institutions' awareness that programmes are entering the viewers' home under their aegis means that there is little likelihood that anything will be broadcast which could be found to be obscene in the courts. Instead, television regulation, which is far more censorious than that conducted by the BBFC on film and video, bases itself on ideas about conscious mass audience reactions rather than the notionally long-term effect of representations on individual psyches.

In 1987, a BBC committee of departmental heads met to update the Corporation's guidelines on violence in programming for producers. These guidelines begin with the way images accompanying television news stories should be selected. Although this pack largely confines itself to the way fiction is regulated, the way television news deals with images of violence in news and current affairs programmes offers a useful point of comparison, and elements from these guidelines are reproduced in Information Sheet 16 (p. 87). The ITC follows similar guidelines for the ITV network, particularly regarding the nine o'clock watershed.

It is clearly the case that we, as television, film and video viewers, judge images according to their varying proximities to our idea of the real world – very few viewers,

The Board has always believed that the deprave-and-corrupt test was the best and most appropriate means of controlling the sort of sadistic entertainment which, as the Williams Committee put it,

> seemed to have no purpose or justification other than to reinforce or sell the idea that it can be highly pleasurable to inflict injury, pain or humiliation (often in a sexual context) on others. (Williams, 12.10)

The Board's interpretation of the deprave-and-corrupt test, as put to the Home Office in our Response to Williams in 1980, was that it could most appropriately be applied to material which

> depicts or describes violence or sexual activity or crime in such a manner as, when taken as a whole, to encourage the imitation or toleration of seriously harmful or criminal behaviour in a significant proportion of those who are likely, having regard to all the circumstances, to read, see or hear it.

This is still the interpretation we apply, and it is this element of immoral influence which seemed to us to be lacking from the DPP's guidelines, particularly with regard to the moral position of the film-maker towards his own material. We would therefore add some further questions to those put by the DPP:

- Is the sympathy of the film-maker on the side of the victim or the aggressor?
- Is the process of the violence indulged in for its own sake, rather than to tell us anything significant about the motives or state of mind of the persons involved?
- Does the camerawork or editing belie the ostensible moral stance of the film by seeking to enlist or encourage our vicarious enjoyment of the film?

(from the BBFC Annual Report, 1988)

adult or children, are likely to become upset by the violence in cartoons like *Tom & Jerry*, and television news is likely to upset viewers more than a violent feature film, no matter how naturalistic the film. These 'modality' judgments lead us to react more strongly as viewers to television news than to drama because television news aspires to be a closer representation of real events. In the classification case study on *Platoon* which follows, for example, one of the examiners who viewed it felt that its closeness to memories of television news coverage of the Vietnam war gave it greater impact. Knowledge and experience brought to a film can affect how an audience member reads or responds to a film – a Vietnam war veteran's reading of *Platoon* would presumably vary according to the film's closeness to the individual memory of the lived events to which it refers.

Research into violence on television

Research conducted by American academics Gerbner and Signorielli into American television over a period of more than twenty years suggested that rather than making viewers more likely to become violent, it could serve to make them more fearful. While viewers enjoy television violence, the overall picture revealed that a television schedule with a preponderance of fictional crime programmes containing depictions of violence tended to make viewers overestimate the likelihood of becoming a victim of real-life violence and provoke feelings of insecurity and vulnerability. Barrie Gunter's research into violence on television concluded that images of violence are most upsetting to viewers and are most likely to produce the result indicated by Gerbner and Signorielli the closer the fictional setting came to the surroundings of the viewer. Gunter linked some of the considerations discussed so far – genre, character motivation, and type of depicted violence – in order to isolate the kind of fiction likely to produce anxiety in viewers. These factors are laid out in a simplified chart in Information Sheet 17 (p. 88). When the Broadcasting Standards Council was set up in 1988, its first task was to produce a code for the portrayal of violence and set up standards of taste and decency on television. A year after the Code was put in place a monograph on violence in television fiction was published by the BSC. BSC research surveyed viewers of different ages and backgrounds in mainland Britain and Northern Ireland and, among other approaches, it compared respondent's views on violence in real life with depictions of violence on television. This researcher's conclusions sum up the difficulties of this area of investigation in the impossibility of easy, 'right' answers to the problems of audiences and images of violence:

> It is clear that no uniform attitude to violent images exists in the UK. Even in Northern Ireland, with all its distinctive experiences, some viewers despised real-life violence but enjoyed greatly fictional violence.
>
> In Britain, the research revealed that many viewers who were committed to methods of violent punishment disliked intensely the representation of such discipline on television. Other respondents vehemently opposed violent punishments but were content to see them appear in a television fiction. Moreover many people were deeply concerned that they may be attacked in their homes but clearly enjoyed war films or horror movies; others felt secure and safe but hated violent films.   Doherty, 1990, p. 37 (see Appendix II p. 27).

BBC TV Producers' Guidelines on Violence in BBC – Produced Drama

- Television drama must be able to reflect important issues truthfully, and violence is part of both nature and society.

- In every era, the often violent clash of good and evil has been the concern of the storyteller.

- Drama on television involves the collaboration of many different skills and creative talents; in any collaboration there must be editorial judgement.

- In all its drama productions, the BBC retains the right, subject to contracts, to make final editorial decisions.

- In the preparation of a production, the producer is responsible for all aspects of the programme.

- It is the responsibility of the producer, assisted by the script editor, to agree with the author a script which can be broadcast. The producer must be aware of the author's contractual rights. These allow minor changes to the script to be made by the producer, but structural alterations need the author's consent.

- Aspects of the production involving violence should be identified and discussed in advance by the producer, the author, and the director, and it is a first priority that any problems in this area must be resolved.

- If in any doubt the producer must refer to the Head of Department, who will, if necessary refer to the Channel Controller or Director of Programmes.

(1983)

Perceptions of Level of Violence in Differing Narrative Contexts

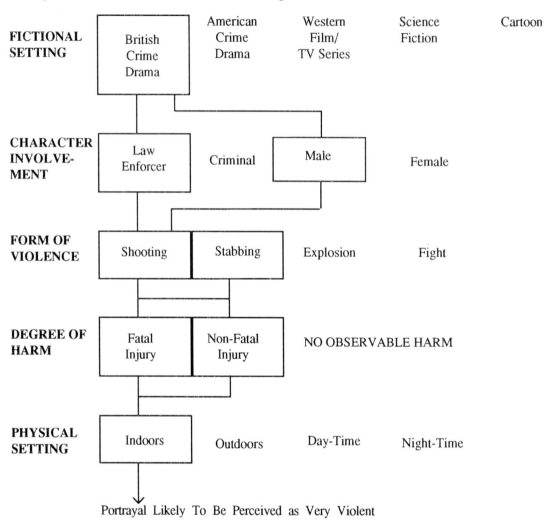

Portrayal Likely To Be Perceived as Very Violent

Background to *Platoon*: regulation and teenage audiences

The Vietnam war film *Platoon* lends itself to a study of the regulation of images of violence on the screen because:

(a) its main classification issue on its release as a film was the suitability of its depiction of violence for teenagers;
(b) the depictions of violence in *Platoon* have a distinct set of narrative, historical and genre contexts, the importance of which can be measured by the students against the more abstract concerns about representations of violence investigated in Activity 8, (p. 74).

No classroom documentation is provided here to place either the subject matter of *Platoon* or the film itself in a historical context – as a relatively recent film, it may be familiar to many of the students and factual material about the Vietnam war is readily available. It may be counterproductive to provide background initially, as a central question concerning audience response relates to how an audience's prior knowledge affects its reading of a text. The film's internal narrative is important and the synopsis on Information Sheet 18 (p. 90) can be used to provide a narrative context for the extract or jog the memory of those students who have seen it. (Alternatively, the students can be asked to watch the whole film.) Students could be asked later to compile articles and reviews on the film from different sources – either from its release on film in 1987 or from its transmission, uncut, on television in December 1991, and/or to provide some background historical material on the Vietnam war. The relevant initial questions for the students to begin to discuss the classification of *Platoon* as a 'violent' film is not 'how much do you know about the Vietnam war?' but 'how much do you think the film expects you to know?' Does the film address audiences with knowledge of the historical background to its narrative differently to audiences who do not have this knowledge? Conversely, are audiences with background knowledge likely to read the film differently? Are younger people more or less knowledgeable about the Vietnam war than older people? Would the representations of violence in the film then be more or less of a worry if the film were classified for teenagers?

Plot Synopsis of *Platoon* (1986): Video Extract Highlighted

Vietnam 1967. Chris Taylor (Charlie Sheen) joins an American Infantry Regiment posted near the Cambodian border. Sent out on a night-time detail to ambush Vietcong soldiers before he has been acclimatised, Chris is wounded and two men are killed when another new recruit, Junior, sleeps on his watch. Three months after his arrival, Chris and the platoon discover an abandoned Vietcong bunker and two platoon members are killed by a bomb left behind in it. The company's lieutenant, Wolfe, is weak and the command of the platoon is split between Sergeant Elias (Willem Dafoe) and Sergeant Barnes (Tom Berenger); the former, a tough but sensitive figure, the latter, a battle-scarred and hardened soldier.

The platoon discover the body of a missing GI impaled on a tree. Under the vengeful Barnes's command, the platoon marches into a Vietnamese village where the villagers are rounded up and supplies of rice and guns are discovered. Emotionally disturbed at the death of the impaled GI, Chris shoots at the feet of an apparently mentally handicapped young man he has discovered hiding underground in a hut. Bunny, a volatile and dangerous youth, beats the young man to death with his rifle butt. Outside, Barnes interrogates the head of the village, threatening his daughter, and when this causes the girl's mother to become hysterical, Barnes shoots her in the head. Elias arrives with his detail and a fight ensues between the two sergeants, ending with Elias telling Barnes he will report the atrocity. The men are ordered to torch the village by Lt. Wolfe. As Chris and the platoon leave, he stops a group of soldiers from raping a village girl. Some of the soldiers carry the children away from the burning village on their shoulders.

Back at the camp the platoon is divided, some following Barnes, the other Elias. When they return to the bunker, Wolfe makes a mistake which means that some of the platoon are killed by their own supporting artillery. Elias, in the confusion, is shot by Barnes who tells Chris he is dead. From a helicopter as they are airlifted out, Chris watches, anguished, as Elias appears on the ground being chased and then killed by enemy soldiers. At the camp, Chris attacks Barnes, but Barnes is stronger. During the next engagement near the Cambodian border, the platoon is decimated and Chris shoots the wounded Barnes in cold blood, his own life being saved by an airstrike and airlift in the area.

A Describe the main events of the extract, including who the main characters are and how they are involved in the events on screen.

(i) Is it possible, if you had only seen this extract and had no further information, to say what the plot of *Platoon* was about? Describe what the extract tells us about:

- Barnes
- Elias
- Bunny
- Chris

(ii) Write a brief description of the sequence from the perspective of each of the above characters. Compare these descriptions. Will the violence which occurs appear different from these perspectives? Which of them is closest to the way the film tells this part of the story?

(iii) If we think of a film's narrative as conforming to the following pattern:

[initial description -> conflict -> resolution]

Can we see the extract as a mini-story? Describe what the various stages in the story would be.

B Do you think the way the violence is set up and filmed in this sequence to be effective? How else could the various elements – special effects, use of cameras – have been used? How would these changes affect the way audiences see the film?

(i) How would this violence probably have been presented, do you think, if *Platoon* were:

- a horror film?
- a TV comedy drama about war (e.g. *M.A.S.H.*)?
- a comic-book action film like *Rambo*?
- any other type of film?

C When audience members see a film which has upset them they sometimes write to the BBFC to complain. Here is an example of the type of letter which is sometimes received:

Dear Sir,

I recently went to see the '15'-rated film *Platoon*. I believe it is inappropriate that the classification of *Platoon* allows it to be seen by 15-year-old children. I would accept that the scenes of extreme violence in the film are in keeping with the nature and intent of the film, but I think it is very wrong that they are seen by children aged 15. I do not feel that young people of this age have the necessary discernment to understand why the violence is part of the film and that, for many, these scenes would merely be extremely distressing and disturbing. I trust you would agree that 15 is still a very impressionable age and I certainly would not want either of my children to be able to see such a film until they were adults.

Yours sincerely
J. Smith

(i) How would you reply to this letter? Draft brief responses to it individually, then compare it to replies drafted by other pupils.

Activity 10 Textual analysis of extract from *Platoon*

Aim

- To develop students' skills in textual analysis in relation to a media text containing depictions of violence.

Objective

- Students should be able to examine different subject positions in the viewing of a media text which could be seen as controversial.

You will need

An extract from *Platoon*, Activity Sheet 7 (p. 91) and Information Sheet 18 (p. 90). The start and end of the extract is identified in the information sheet.

What you do

Screen the extract in class and discuss the students' reactions. Focus the discussion around the way the extract mediates the horrific events it depicts, with the help of Activity Sheet 7. The students should be divided into small groups to consider one of the questions on the sheet. The questions are in three parts: A, B and C.

A aims at encouraging the students to discuss how the extract constructs its narrative, through considerations of point of view and narrative development;
B deals with the question of the extract's depiction of violence;
C invites study of potential audience responses and each student's personal views compared with others.

Activity 11 *Platoon* and teenage audiences: classroom debate on regulating images of violence

Aim

- To promote a critical knowledge and understanding of the way aspects of audience, narrative and genre affect the age classification of a media text.

Objective

- Students should be able to use discussion of the processes by which *Platoon* was classified in the '15' category by the BBFC to stimulate debate on the question of teenage audiences and depictions of violence in media texts.

Background

Information Sheet 19 (p. 95) contains brief responses selected from BBFC examiners' reports on the film. These have been chosen because they encapsulate issues presented by the extract contained in the accompanying video and discuss the depiction of violence in this scene in terms of the possible reactions of prospective audiences aged fifteen to seventeen years old. The selection of passages from longer reports like this does not fully do justice to the work of the examiners concerned, just as the isolating of the sequence on the video cannot replace the experience of *Platoon* as a film. It almost goes without saying, given what is discussed in these report extracts, that the sequence in the accompanying video could be upsetting to some members of the class. These reports were written after the various screenings of the film at the Board in January 1987. Many examiners and members of the Board who saw the film believed it to be suitable only for eighteen-year-olds and above, but most regretted the fact that fifteen-year-olds would be barred from a film that they were likely to find interesting. Further screenings followed and the distribution company was informed of the probable '18' classification. The film distributor appealed to the BBFC to review this decision having had a change of mind about the desired category for the film following an appeal by the Australian distributor, who had successfully argued the distinction between *Platoon* and the recently released cycle of comic-book war heroics films like the Chuck Norris *Missing in Action* series and the *Rambo* films.

The Director of the BBFC decided to organise a test screening in order to gain some empirical evidence to place the possible responses of the teenage audience suggested by the examiners.

What you need
Information Sheet 19 and Information Sheet 20 (pp. 95 and 96), which contains questions from the questionnaire used at the test screenings of *Platoon* to try and establish the responses of teenage audiences, may be of use in stimulating initial classroom discussion.

What you do
Distribute the quotations on Information Sheet 19 to the students. It may be productive to distribute these, one to a group, and have the students discuss how far they agree with the sentiments expressed, placing the emphasis on justifying their arguments and opinions rather than relying on simple assertion. Activity Sheet 8 (p. 97) contains questions which may be of use in focusing discussion on the question of differing audience readings of media texts. These aim to build on the textual analysis in the previous activity and on the general work on audiences in Activities 1-3 (pp. 35-45).

Notes
Test screenings are increasingly performed in Hollywood by production companies. The question being posed by these screenings is whether the film would appeal to target audiences, providing them with the requisite pleasures to transform the film into a money spinner. Films are sometimes then cut or re-edited to conform with the findings of these screenings. This has occurred with action films in order to test whether a target audience of young men are going to be bored between the action scenes. This can be discussed as another example of economic self-censorship. Test screenings to assess the suitability of *Platoon* for mid-teenagers by the BBFC were organised initially for a group of teachers who gave their views on the possible success of a test screening with young people. When the film was subsequently test-screened like this, a questionnaire was completed following the viewing. This questionnaire aimed at testing the various propositions found in examiners' reports about the potential range of teenage responses to the film. The aim was to find out, for example, if the film was simply 'more bang to the buck' as the *Time* magazine passage quoted in Examiner Report 3, that is to say whether some audiences would respond to it as primarily an action film like the *Rambo* films. Or whether it would have distinct general meanings about war, atrocity and moral responsibility for young people, which would place the intense depiction of violence in the film in a more secure context from the point of view of the censor.

There were ninety-four teenagers at the screening, split evenly by gender and ranging from fifteen to seventeen. Two of the questions, 3 and 4, connect with the general considerations about violence in the media introduced briefly in the first part of this section of the workbook. They ask the young audience to make decisions about the possible responses of others, the results were:

- Do you think other people would like the film?
  Yes   95 per cent
  No   4 per cent
- Do you think anyone would find it upsetting?
  Yes   87 per cent
  No   4 per cent

This leads to the conclusion that, in the view of the teenage respondents, people would like the film either in spite of or because of the fact that it was upsetting. When asked for the possible cause of audiences being upset, pleasurably or otherwise, the proportion of the sample who had replied 'yes' gave as their reasons:

- violence   73.5 per cent
- the Battles   36.5 per cent
- drug taking   11   per cent
- bad language   26   per cent

The conclusion is that the simple message summed up in the cliché 'war is hell' is an easily understood one. War in *Platoon* presents itself to the teenage audience as a situation in which moral decisions are magnified to an almost hyperbolic extent – something which is clear in the extract's progress from the protagonists' confusion, through passivity to saving the young villager from being gang-raped by the soldiers. In this context, the teenagers seemed to be saying, violence should be allowed to be upsetting.

Discussion of this rather straightforward conclusion can be deepened, though, by raising the question of how far this result illustrates the more contentious observation that concern over images of violence in films tends to take place on an abstract level: films with representations of violence are often popular with audiences who, when questioned, often claim to be against 'media violence'.

Extracts from BBFC examiners' reports on *Platoon*

1. It is stronger than anything in *The Killing Fields,* and could be seriously disturbing (or worse, exciting) to even the most *Rambo*-hardened 15-year-old. The torturing of the helpless Vietnamese man who is forced to dance by having bullets fired at his feet, the shot of the baby-faced Bunny laughing in sadistic glee, and above all the close up of the rifle-butt crashing into the victim's skull, followed by Bunny's excited gabble ('Hey shit, did you see that fucking head come apart? I never seen brains spilt like that – let's fucking do the old women, let's do the whole village!). Is this really the kind of material we should be passing at '15'? My answer, on the basis of my own experience of teenagers' endurance and sensibility, must be 'NO'. This scene, horrors of war or not, is simply too strong for '15'.

2. I am part of a generation who watched (protested vicariously against) the progress of the war in Vietnam. I am also part of a generation who watched, also in slightly late adulthood, filmic expressions of horror after the war was lost by America, which were considered unquestionably adult material – *Apocalypse Now* and *The Deer Hunter*. *Platoon* therefore makes harrowing sense to me. With that experience and in that context, the physical violence and inhuman abuse in the film are seen in a framework of knowledge and with an assumption of maturity. Without either the vicarious experience of the war as an adult knowledge of the roots of violence, the stimuli for abuse, an individual's retreat from human compassion, the driving necessity of an institution (war, the army) of cloning its participants in its own image so as to ensure total obedience, the film's images are of simple human damage. (*sic*)

3. *Platoon* is the best film I've seen on the Vietnam War – and the use of Samuel Barber's Adagio for strings is a real tear-jerker. The film tells us nothing about the Vietnamese but it says so much about the nightmare of American involvement. ... The distributor's request for an '18' category should be granted ... I would have considered the '15' but the above expletive count and specific visuals convince me that the correct category for this film is '18'. One final reason for the '18' is contained in the following critique. *Time* magazine, 26/1/87, comments that *Platoon* offers something for everyone: The army of *Rambo*-maniacs will love the picture because it delivers more bang for the buck; all those yellow folk blow up real good. Ageing lefties can see the film as a demonstration of war's inhuman futility. Greybeards on the right may call it a tribute to our fighting men, in whatever foreign adventure. The intelligentsia can credit *Platoon* with expressing Stone's grand theories of comradeship and betrayal. And the average youthful moviegoer ... may discover where Dad went in the 60s and why he came home changed or came home in a body bag. You 'pays your money', you take what message you want. It is best placed in the adult category.

4. The rights of citizens under 18 seem non-existent. That I accept as a given state of things and I am only provoked into registering my resistance when arguments for our classification system as baldly stated as they were in our discussion – that the '15' for *Platoon* would not ring the appropriate alarm bells for little old ladies over 50 who would be expecting a softer touch from that category and would not be sufficiently prepared for that experience. Just who are we protecting here?

5. None of us could doubt that there are some teenagers who would both enjoy and learn from this important film. The unspoken gender element re-occurs here – this is massively a film that will appeal to boys. The fear is that some 'lads' when they get together in the cinema may misuse this film, as it were, as another 'get the gooks' *Rambo* experience. Though I might well be saddened by that personally, it would not be very high in my list of reasons for going for the '18'. Not only because I might well have done that in similar company at that age myself, but more because such group pressures are contradictory. A 'lad' may be larking around and getting off on all the 'wrong things' on the surface and being moved and educated underneath. Still, once the film is being consumed at that more uncritically macho level it does militate against more mature responses. Even at '18' these kind of contradictions will occur, but at least we will have acted more consistently, I feel ...

Questionnaire on *Platoon*

1. What did you think of the film? (Stated replies: exciting, frightening, confusing, enjoyable, boring, makes you think, horrifying, rubbish.)

2. Were there any parts of the film you didn't like?

3. Do you think other people would like this film?

4. Do you think anyone would find it upsetting? If yes, who?

5. Have you seen any of the following films?

   Rambo; Missing in Action; The Killing Fields; Mad Max 3; Apocalypse Now; Commando; The Deerhunter:

6. How did *Platoon* compare with … (better/not as good/ the same)?

7. (i) Do you like war movies?
   (ii) Was this a typical war movie?

8. Which bits of the film do you remember?

9. Why do you remember those bits?

10. What do you think of the main character?

11. Which character in the film did you identify with? Why?

12. Which other characters did you like? Why?

13. Which characters didn't you like? Why?

14. Who was the enemy? Did you recognise them?

15. Would you go to see this film again?

16. Would you tell your friend to go and see it?

17. How would you describe it to your friend?

18. What is the youngest age that should see it?

19. Any other comment about the film?

TEENAGE AUDIENCES AND DEPICTIONS OF VIOLENCE

Extracts from BBFC examiners' reports on *Platoon*

1. The BBFC examiners always see sequences like the one from *Platoon* in the context of the whole film. Do you think it is important to see the whole film before discussing the age of the audiences for which it may be suitable? Give reasons for your answer.

2. Do you think different people respond to films in different ways? For example, do you think teenagers see films differently from people in their twenties, thirties or even older? Do you think men and women, boys and girls, see films differently? Ask your parents or guardians, friends, fellow students both older and younger about what they think of recent films you and they have seen.

   - Do you think there are subjects which occur in films which are unsuitable for certain age groups?
   - Do you feel that you have seen films recently which you would have understood differently when you were younger?
   - Do films in your view tend to appeal to 'target audiences' or do you think there are films which appeal to everyone, no matter what their age, gender or knowledge of the world?

3. Do you think the *Rambo* films and *Platoon* could appeal to the same audiences? Are there audiences who would enjoy them both for the same or different reasons?

4   Sexual imagery and young audiences: Madonna

Introduction

Sexual imagery in the classroom

Discussing and investigating representations of sex in films and videos and the way various regulatory authorities respond to them is an extremely difficult classroom task. Calls for censorship of film, video and television images of sex come from various quarters: from moral campaigners like the National Viewers' and Listeners' Association who hold the view that representations of sex should be heavily censored for adults and kept away from children and adolescents because such images could destabilise the nuclear family and the Christian values to which large sections of Britain's population adhere; and also from certain (but certainly not all) feminist positions, which hold that images of sex can degrade women and contribute to sexual inequality and even real violence towards women. In many ways, debates around these issues are of great importance to the way film and video is regulated in Britain and what images of sex are allowed on television, given that regulations are expected to reflect all shades of public opinion in their decisions. The various pornography debates are difficult to deal with at this level and there are good reasons why sexual material which is contentious for adults should not be brought into the classroom. It suffices to indicate that, despite the liberalisation in representations of sex and sexuality which accompanied the social changes of the 60s, Britain is still the most heavily censored country in Europe, apart from Ireland, when it comes to pornography on film and video.

Images of sex in the context of non-sex material – i.e. 'love scenes' – in films are, however, dealt with largely by classification rather than censorship. This is one of a number of distinctions which can and should be made to allow some of the issues underlying such regulation to be discussed by pupils, given the fact that it is indisputable that adolescents are now brought into contact with more sexual imagery from a wider variety of sources than previous generations. The main distinctions are between (i) pornography; (ii) sex within the context of film, video and television fictions; and (iii) representations of sex in still photographic image, for example in advertising. Although the definitions of pornography are widely contested, we can define it here as material which has, as its primary purpose, the sexual arousal of the viewer. Its production, circulation and consumption remains a source of controversy and concern in Britain and although the reasons why this is the case are central to why material grouped under (ii) above is regulated according to the age of the prospective audience, it is more effective to approach the topic from the perspective of images which the students are likely either to encounter or seek out for reasons which may be entirely separate from those which prompt some adults to wish to view pornography.

In choosing a case study for this part of the study pack, then, the main criteria were:

- material with which the pupils are likely to be familiar
- material which addresses a teenage audience;
- material which uses sexual imagery or part of this mode of address; and
- material which because of this is controversial.

If we consider sequences representing sex from films aimed at young people – for example *The Delinquents* (Australia, Chris Thomson, 1989), passed '12', or *Ghost* (US, Jerry Zucker, 1990), also passed '12', or such '15'-rated films as *An Officer and a Gentleman* (US, Taylor Hackford, 1982) – the problems of isolating sequences in the form of an extract become apparent. A simple measure of the 'acceptability' of sequences involving representations of sex is how far the audience is involved with the characters, whether the scene contains information about the characters. This sounds like a reiteration of the censor's concern over images of violence described in the last section, but there is a difference. There, 'context-less' violence was merely hypothesised, here 'context-less' representations of sexual activity clearly exist in the form of pornography. To show sequences of sexual imagery out of context is thus to shuffle them in the direction of the pornographic, and one often-remarked-upon aspect of video as a medium is that it lends itself readily to such use.

Far more productive, because far less potentially alienating for the students and difficult for the teacher, is to use material whose viewing contexts may even be more apparent to the pupils than to their parents or the teacher, so that the initial challenge of discerning the possible meanings of the images should be one the pupils are equipped to meet. For example, rock videos satisfy the four criteria listed above.

Pop videos and sexual imagery

The list of the type of media products which could include sexual imagery does not include pop videos as such. As a form, the pop video could be considered in various ways – as, for example, a video fiction or an advertisement for an audio recording. One commentator, theorising about the different relationship between the visual and the aural in film and video as media, makes the following observation about pop videos:

> The pop video is … a form in which the standard assumptions of visual predominance in an audiovisual medium no longer apply. The key commercial element is clearly the music. Moreover since this music is itself a studio product which probably cannot be reproduced by live performers in concert, there can often be no question of the use of the normal techniques for subordinating sound through synchronisation (so that the image seems to produce the sound). The result is a form which is both fascinating and self-contradictory: distributed in video format but shot on film, free-wheeling yet constrained by its advertising function,

> visually innovative yet subordinated to its soundtrack, an individual artifact which is parasitic in a separate and commercially more important object (the record or cassette), a part of the distinctive youth culture that needs to be played through the equipment forming the focus of family life. Despite – or perhaps because of – these contradictions – the pop video points to the new potential of video as a medium in its own right. (Armes, Roy, *On Video*, London, Routledge, 1988, pp. 157-8.)

The pop video as a form is often traced back to the success of a video made by the rock band Queen in 1976 for their single 'Bohemian Rhapsody', but it has forerunners in the short films made for jazz jukeboxes in the 30s. Pop videos developed in the late 70s and the 80s due to the arrival of cable and satellite television music channels in the USA and later Britain, particularly the MTV channel, most of whose programming is made up of pop videos. They are often shown on children's television on *Top of the Pops* and other teen and pre-teen oriented 'youth' programming. They are also sold as pre-recorded videograms – a popular form of video purchase because they have the important quality of replayability. A worldwide survey of video usage in the mid-80s pointed out that:

> Possibly the most significant single area of videogram sale is that of pop music videos. Certainly the production of these tapes has had a stimulating effect on the British independent film industry. In 1984, for example, 800 pop videos were made in the United Kingdom at a cost of approximately 12 million making the country the second largest in this field in the world (the United States produced nearly 2,000 in the same year – France and the Federal Republic each produced 100). Sales are substantial and as with records, a weekly 'hot' sales chart is compiled. (Alvarado, 1988, p. 11.)

1984 was also the year of the passing of the Video Recordings Act. Generally, music videos, like video games, are exempt from the Act because they are 'concerned with sport, religion or music' (other exempt videos are those 'designed to inform, educate or instruct'). Some exempt works will carry an 'e' on the cover in place of a category symbol. Section 2(2) of the Act removes the exempt status, however, if the video 'to any significant extent' depicts:

- human sexual activity or acts of force or restraint associated with such activity;
- mutilation or torture of, or other gross violence towards, humans or animals;
- human genital organs or human urinary or excretory functions.*

(* does not include videos used for medical training as these are 'exempted supply'.)

Only a few of the hundreds of music videos released in Britain are submitted for classification and these tend to be the ones which have either been found by the distribution company to contain elements which they fear may cause complaint from viewers if they were unclassified, or touch on the areas listed above. They may also submit tapes if they discover that they contain bad language, drug-taking, nudity or if the tape has already caused controversy in other forms of distribution on television, for example. Many tapes featuring American rap bands such as NWA and 2 Live Crew fall into this category, some rap music audio records having caused some controversy in the United States. *Justify My Love* had already come to the notice of the press, due to the controversy over its screening on MTV and the decision of the BBC's *Top of the Pops* not to screen the video in late 1990. Tabloid articles stressing the 'sexiness' of the video and presaging the enormous hype accorded Madonna's British tour and subsequent film, *In Bed With Madonna* (US, Alek Keshishian, 1991), passed '18' on film and video by the BBFC. Following from the screening of the video on a late-night youth television programme, the BSC's Code of Practice contains two references to pop videos. In the section 'Sex and Sexuality' under a subheading, 'Lyrics, Television and Radio', it states:

Pop videos which combine music with mini-dramas should observe the limits applied to drama, having in mind the different times at which they are likely to be transmitted. The precise time of scheduling all pop videos should be chosen with care. (BSC, *A Code of Practice*, London, 1989, p. 40.)

The section referring to drama points out that 'it is over the representation of sexual activity in televised or filmed drama that the most enduring controversies have arisen in recent years', and exhorts producers to consider context with care, so that the audience is not 'reduced to the level of voyeurs' (p. 38). As with most forms of regulation of images it is stressed that context is all-important, but what kind of contexts are relevant for pop videos? Pop video is a form which clearly addresses young viewers and it is often the media product that provides the model for young people when they are given the opportunity to work with video production equipment at school or college. This is a useful form, then, for examining depictions of sexuality in the classroom, in order to focus critical thought on the part of the students on how images of sex can be packaged for them, how controversy over sexual imagery can fulfil promotional and advertising functions within the marketplace and where regulation does or should fit into this picture.

Activity 12   Background discussion

Discussion of images of sexuality and the teenage audience.

Aims

- To encourage students to think critically about the way images of sexuality address them in media texts.
- To promote critical consideration of the role of such representations in the marketing of popular media texts.

Objective

- Students should be able to validate their own knowledge of the Madonna phenomenon and use it to inform a wider discussion of regulation of sexual imagery for a teenage audience.

What you need
A copy of Madonna's *Justify My Love* video sleeve, Information Sheets 21 and 8 (pp. 102 and 62-3).

What you do
In order to establish and put to classroom use the students' passive knowledge about Madonna – knowledge which will have possibly been increased by the immense publicity and controversy generated by her book *Sex* – ask the students to analyse and discuss the possible meanings of the image taken from a video sleeve of *Justify My Love*, and compare their discussion of this with the video sleeve of *The Wild One* on Information Sheet 8. The discussion should focus naturally primarily on questions of gender:

- What does it mean, for example, to note that Madonna has borrowed a style from a male star of the 50s?
- Do male audiences see Madonna differently to female audiences?

In order to provide a springboard for class discussion, Information Sheet 21 contains quotations about Madonna from the welter of press attention accorded her during 1991, and students could be asked to gather press material from the 'controversy' about Madonna's publicity.

QUOTATIONS ABOUT MADONNA'S USE OF SEXUALITY

1. Madonna never does anything for publicity. Rather publicity is the language naturally used by the great stars to communicate with their vast audience. Through publicity we live in the star's flowing consciousness.

(Camille Paglia, *Independent on Sunday,* 21 July 1991)

2. Madonna's appeal is universal, she is a phenomenon of her times, like 'safe sex'. Beyond that, she is a reminder that the age gets the artists, or at least the artificers it deserves. With Madonna, what you see – the clothes, the snarls, the simpers – is what you get: what you hear is hype.

(Profile, *Sunday Telegraph,* 19 May 1991)

3. She can adopt any image of womanhood – a whore, a porn model, a nun or Marilyn Monroe – but these images never constrict her. They are merely images plucked off the rail, open for play and parody. When Madonna adopts the attire of bondage and masturbates on stage, it is the audience who is manipulated, not the powerful wealthy women on the stage. ... [However] play and parody may have entered the fashion arena but this has failed to dislodge fundamental unevenness between men and women's relationships to sexual display and adornment. Women are still more concerned than men with rendering themselves sexually desirable and conforming to prevailing ideals ... her sexual appeal is no less fed up with expressing current 'female' values than, say, the ideal of feminine passivity of the 1950s. The message Madonna's clothes and body give is more complex, but it does nothing to break the age-old assumption that women's power *is* sex. ... It may be that there is not such an enormous gulf between a woman of the Fifties and a woman of the Nineties, if the identities of both are tied up in a sexual sell.

(Ros Coward, 'Madonna on Marilyn's perilous peroxide path', *Observer,* 5 May 1991)

Activity 13 Textual analysis and discussion of the classification

Background

The video classification of 'Justify My Love'

When the video containing 'Justify My Love' was submitted to the BBFC for classification, the Board had to decide which age group it was suitable for. The BBFC's practice concerning sexual images at '15' is to measure degree of explicitness against the narrative context, to ask the question, 'what is this sex scene saying about the characters and about sex to young people?' If the sex scene is only there to provide voyeuristic pleasure then it is generally passed '18'. The way representations of sexual imagery are shot is also important – the body parts the camera appears interested in, the length of time shots are held and the selection of close-ups. With pop videos, these considerations – of editing and *mise en scène* – are complicated by the form's unique approach to balancing narrative and images and subordinating them largely to the music. Can this be in the words of the BSC Code of Practice, for example, a 'mini-drama'?

Pupils could be asked to produce a brief narrative synopsis outlining a possible story of the video. How far is this a creative-writing exercise? The group could be asked to assess how much of the story they were having to invent to identify characters, explain motivation, etc. To what extent do the lyrics define the imagery? How much does the music and vocal soundtrack influence the context, style and pace of the imagery and narrative.

A further line of investigation could focus on the idea that pop videos rely as much on visual performance or narrative. Here the performance could be seen to relate to Madonna's stage shows, which have themselves been controversial, the costumes and dance routines being seen as sexually suggestive. How far is this video also about dance? The movements and editing have obviously been choreographed for the music, which, as the earlier quotation by Armes suggests, takes precedence over the visuals. Does the sexual imagery have to be measured against these considerations. Does this make the imagery itself more abstract?

Information Sheet 22 (p. 105) contains brief extracts from BBFC examiners' reports attempting to grapple with the suitability of this video for fifteen-year-olds. Twelve examiners and officers of the BBFC saw this video and the decision was finally for the '18' certificate even though it was concluded that the intention and effect of the images in context was to provoke rather than titillate. The distributor also wanted an '18' certificate, presumably to capitalise on the selling power of the controversy surrounding the television screening.

Aims

- To position the student in the role of regulator with regard to representations of sexuality in a pop video, and other film and video texts.

Objective

- To consider the relationship between the institutional regulatory bodies, the British 'public' consciousness and age-related classification and censorship.

What you need

A copy of the Madonna video 'Justify My Love' and the video clip material from the 'Nudity' section, Information Sheet 22 (p. 105) and Activity Sheet 9 (p. 106).

What you do

Distribute the sheets and use them as the basis of a classroom debate. The students can be canvassed first on their initial suggestions for the classification of the tape: either 'U', 'PG', '15' or '18'. Split the students into groups according to their initial choice of classification. Then have each group, through debate amongst themselves, come up with as many reasons as possible to justify their decision. Each group should then report back and the discussion be opened out to the whole group.

Examiners' comments

1. The first song's sexy contents, and the '18' requested, should not be the end of the '15'/'18' debate, because (a) this is a pop song, (b) the sexy images are brief moments (the iconography of Madonna's 'kinkiness' which 'everyone knows' and recognises as her trademark), and (c) the cross-dressing, gender confusion style is part of the pop world's presentation. Does it have to be '18'? I would like others to view before we go for the '18', but would make a plea that no fifteen-year-old would worry a jot about this. Parents may frown.

2. All in all, given Madonna's reputation, fairly predictable and not at all outrageous. Anyone buying a Madonna video will expect a bit of sexual teasing. This is not quite strong '18' stuff (company requests '18') and would be acceptable at '15'.

3. As $9^1/_2$ *Weeks* moved the '18' sex scene in the direction of the pop promo, this travels in the opposite direction, introducing soft-core images (which are probably alien to Madonna's audience of young teenage girls) which, even in the context of a rock video, would be unprecedented at '15'.

   Given that the public controversy over this is already under way (Radio DJs, for example, who are forced to play this single because of its popularity, talk all the way through it, and, on one occasion, I have heard, actually call it rubbish in order to 'detoxify' it for the radio audience).

   It strikes me that we have very good reasons for not throwing caution to the wind on images of three-way sex and '18' level images clearly directly intended to titillate, as we know that this tape is going to be bought by young teenage, and even pre-teenage girls. We have to worry that when parents see that their young daughter's porn-like Madonna tape – which has been splashed over the tabloids – has the apparent seal of approval of a '15' on the cover, they will see this as a good cause for complaint.

MADONNA, 'JUSTIFY MY LOVE'

1. Do you think that your parents would complain about your younger brother or sister watching this tape? At which age would you allow him or her to watch it?

2. Does 'Justify My Love' tell a story? Write a short outline (synopsis) of the story.

3. Would this video be different if:

   • it were Madonna's first video when she was an unknown drummer in 1979?
   • if you did not recognise:

   i)   the star?
   ii) the song?
   iii) both?

4. Do you think there are ways in which sex should and should not be depicted in films aimed at young audiences? Explain with reference to the following statement:

   Sex in films can be:

   i)   embarrassing;
   ii) interesting;
   iii) put in to sell the film or video;
   iv) educational;
   v)   unnecessary.

5. Can you think of other pop videos that have been controversial? What aspect of them caused controversy?

6. Watch the clips from the video compilation entitled 'Nudity'. The video clips are extracts taken from a "test" tape shown in schools as part of a survey. The clips are taken from:

   a) *Sheena, Queen of the Jungle*   '15'
   b) *The Delinquents*   '12'
   c) *A Room With a View*   'PG'

   Bear in mind these are extracts and they are taken out of context. Discuss the clips using questions 1 and 4, and answer this question:

   What scenes of nudity would you find acceptable in a children's feature film 'U' certificated?

5   Representations of drug misuse in films, videos and on television

Background

Films depicting drug abuse are a perennial concern of censors. John Trevelyan records how, in 1915, images of drugs were banned from films not because drug use was prevalent but because it was felt that such images may arouse curiosity. With the arrival of the 60s and the appearance of drug usage as part of youth counter-culture, it was no longer a question of preventing audiences from gaining 'dangerous knowledge', but rather of preventing films making drugs look attractive. In 1967, a low-budget American film which, in Trevelyan's words 'purported to show the psychedelic experience resulting from LSD', was banned on the advice of psychiatrists who felt it to be 'inaccurate and meretricious'. The enduring nature of this aspect of the censor's job is illustrated by the fact that when this same film was submitted on video in 1988, it was rejected again. The BBFC Annual Report for that year stated:

> This video film was rejected because of its encouragement – verging on advocacy – of drug abuse, in this case LSD, a decision which confirms the previous rejection of this film on three separate occasions. (Ferman, BBFC Annual Report 1988 (1989), p. 14.)

As with other areas of the censor's activities, there are no written rules about when depictions of drug-taking in films are unacceptable. The BBFC's worries about 'advocacy' and 'encouragement' of drug-taking by films links censorship again to the social welfare ethos identified so far in other contexts. The censor measures representations of a social problem against whether these representations are likely to exacerbate that problem, and again the 'how' of representation is as important as the 'what'. The censor's twin concerns from 1912 to the present are whether films either instruct viewers in the use of drugs or in some way – through glamorising, normalising or trivialising them in representation – advocate their use.

Instruction

BBFC practice renders it unacceptable for films and videos to instruct audiences, and removes detailed scenes of characters 'shooting up' (injecting themselves with needles) or other techniques of drug abuse such as 'freebasing' or 'chasing the dragon'. This policy is based both in the personal teaching capability of video with its rewind and pause facilities and in the view that detailed presentations of the process of drug use betray an interest in the process by the film-makers themselves and a pandering to viewers who may, according to James Ferman, become fascinated with this process:

> The drug problem in Britain has assumed epidemic proportions since the publication of the Board's last Annual Report and BBFC policy on drugs has continued to deal very strictly with screen entertainment which seeks to normalise, glamorise or directly advocate the abuse of drugs which are controlled by British law. Such scenes are subject to control, on film as well as video, but video as a domestic medium is subject to stricter standards because of the susceptible individuals and televised scenes of drug preparation and use, which may assume a hypnotic fascination when viewed repeatedly in private. (Ferman, BBFC Annual Report 1987 (1988), p. 11.)

This means that lengthy scenes of 'hard' drug preparation are cut from videos even for adults. Documentaries about drug abuse are exempt from this, but quasi-documentaries like Andy Warhol's *Trash* (US, Paul Morrissey, 1970), which was banned on film in the 70s and is released only in cut form on video, are not and neither is a drama-documentary approach like *Christiane F.* (West Germany, Ulrich Edel,

1981), which had close shots of needles going into veins removed which the censor believed, could produce this 'fascination effect'. Similarly, the Board takes a dim view of films which have positively presented characters describing the benefits of 'hard' drug abuse, which is probably as near to direct advocacy as films could become without transforming themselves into commercials. This is, however, an unlikely 'worst case' scenario although the film (*Christiane F.*) is felt to come close.

Glamorisation

Far more likely and, of course, more debatable, is the idea of 'glamorisation'. It is very often the case that the BBFC will see films which link images of sex, intended to titillate the viewer, with depictions of drug-taking. The message that the censor reads in such scenes – that sexual pleasure and drug abuse are conceptually linked – is one which is removed from films and videos. However, given there are many mitigating factors – soft drugs being less dangerous to the individual and society would not cause as many worries – a depicted link between marijuana use and sex would mean the difference, for example, between '15' and '18'. In many thrillers of the *Miami Vice* and *Scarface* (US, Brian de Palma, 1982) variety, the connection between the glamour and the power achieved by drugs gangsters before their demise is a part of the genre and is found acceptable.

However, the video regulators also believe that drugs can be 'fetishised' by films. 'Fetish' is an anthropological term for an inanimate object which is believed in certain cultures to be the embodiment of a spirit or magical power. In its more abstract usage, it can denote any object or activity to which an individual can become excessively and irrationally devoted. This is the sense in which advertisements for consumer goods can turn the objects they are selling into a signifier of something far more than its function. Cars are an obvious example. Cars in advertising can connote speed, power, sex or even family life. The car itself, of course, has the qualities of a fetish before it becomes an object of

advertisement, it being an object to which many people are 'irrationally devoted' with clear, adverse social consequences. Can films advertise drugs in this way? The BBFC clearly believes so. One examiner report from 1987 describes the opening of a crime thriller about drug smuggling as follows:

> The video opens after a title credit with a bag of cocaine being cut open in close up, the powder being ground with a mortar and pestle, it being pushed into a capillary tube and a man putting it into bags. This is quite problematic as there is no doubt that this opening sequence fetishises the drug with its insistent close ups and lighting which endows the substance with an atmosphere of sensuality. (BBFC Examiner's Report, 1987)

Normalisation

Another concern of the censor in connection with the representation of both 'soft' and 'hard' drugs is the 'normalisation' of drug-taking. If, for example, there is a party scene in which marijuana is seen being smoked and enjoyed with no comment or criticism of this within the film, then this sequence is unlikely to be passed at 'U' or 'PG'. This approach is supported by some of those involved in the treatment of drug abusers. In the mid-80s, for example, the Motion Picture Association of America (MPAA) ratings board was petitioned by film critics and drug rehabilitation organisations to change their approach to the rating of films which feature depictions of drug-taking as normal and enjoyable. One of these organisations was the Scott Newman Center, which was funded by the Hollywood star Paul Newman, following the death of his son from a drug overdose. These gaps listed a series of sixty Hollywood films featuring drugs in some way or other and which had been passed in categories allowing children access to these films. They argued that the MPAA should add the letters 'SA' standing for 'substance abuse' to the ratings given to such films in future. The MPAA refused, its reason being that a move like this would open the doors for other pressure groups to demand additions to the American category system and that parents themselves should be the ones to decide what their children see, except for adult 'NC17' and 'X' material. The campaigners turned to Hollywood producers and scriptwriters to dissuade them from including scenes of casual drug-taking in future. The situation, according to an article in the *New York Daily News* was particularly visible with bought-in films on American television, which is very heavily censored in all other respects:

> Today network television has virtually eliminated positive drugs references from its programming and has produced numerous dramas and series whose themes carry strong anti-drugs messages. But at the same time, the networks continue to screen motion pictures with drugs sequences, even though they edit out obscenity, graphic violence and explicit sexual content. (*New York Daily News, Parade Magazine*, 21 July 1985, p. 5.)

According to BBFC practice, the sequences of drug-taking would have been cut for the lower category or would have been passed '15' if there were other reasons for a prohibitive category. This American example of self-censorship is mentioned in the BBFC's Annual Report for 1989, which also mentions that these moves were part of a larger public policy in the United States:

> The glamorisation of soft drugs is less of a problem these days in American films since the anti-drug campaign of the Reagan presidency led Hollywood producers to look more carefully at whether their films 'sell drugs to kids'. (Ferman, BBFC Annual Report, 1989 (1990), p. 11.)

Trivialisation

BBFC policy also concerns itself with the 'trivialisation' of

drug-taking through depictions in film and videos. Jokes involving soft drugs in films are, like every other application of classification and censorship policies, treated on their merits. For example, in the film comedy *Airplane!* (US, Abrahams, Zucker and Zucker, 1980) there is a series of sight gags which includes a brief shot of an old lady sniffing cocaine which was passed 'PG' as the joke depends on recognition, while in *Modern Times* (US, Charles Chaplin, 1936), Charlie Chaplin becomes comically uncoordinated after sniffing 'nose powder', as the subtitles call it, and this was passed 'U'. *Crocodile Dundee* (Australia, Peter Faiman, 1986), however, had references to cocaine in a joke involving a man sniffing it in a kitchen and being instructed by Paul Hogan to get his head over a bowl of steaming water into which he pours the drug, imagining it to be a medicine. The joke remains, but the identification of the drug was removed for 'PG' on film.

Television is regulated by similar considerations to those to be found in the BSC's Code of Practice, which states:

> A number of feature films is at the very least ambivalent about the use of drugs, implying a degree of tolerance toward the practice. Nothing should be done in programmes to encourage any extension of that attitude of tolerance towards the taking of drugs in Britain or the view that taking them was socially acceptable. This is particularly important in programmes expecting to attract large numbers of young people, who might be expected to model their behaviour on the leading performers. Detailed demonstrations of drug-taking techniques or the mechanics of procuring drugs should, in general, be avoided in fiction and included only after senior editorial decisions have been made. (BSC Code of Practice, 1989, p. 49.)

Alcohol and tobacco can be seen as more socially acceptable drugs, cigarette commercials are banned entirely both on television and in the cinema in Britain. Cinema commercials for cigars, pipe tobacco and snuff are allowed. In 1991, the ITC banned cigar advertising on television but it is still allowed by the BBFC and the Cinema Exhibitors Association (CEA). These advertisements are passed 'PG' and upwards. With alcohol the situation is slightly different – alcohol commericals are still allowed at 'U' and this is regulated by the CEA as well as the BBFC. On video, where the BBFC makes up its own rules, advertisements for spirits are usually passed '18' and beers, lagers and wines are usually passed '15'.

Before any alcohol advertisements arrive to be classified, they are governed by the Drinks Code of the Code of Advertising Practice Committee, a trade association which monitors advertisements and regulates them on a voluntary basis. Sections of the Code as it applies to drink, tobacco and young people are reproduced in Information Sheet 23 (p. 112). Discussions of how tobacco and alcohol are regulated is a good way of focusing classroom discussion on issues around representation of drugs in the media.

Activity 14 Simulation

Devising and analysing a television or cinema commercial for an alcoholic drink.

Aim

• To promote a critical understanding of the ways in which media texts can be thought to affect consumption or abuse of drugs.

Objective

• Students should be able to engage with and become knowledgeable about the ways in which media texts' depiction of drugs are or should be regulated.

What you need

Information Sheet 23 (p. 112) containing the Code of Advertising Practice as it applies to alcohol and young people.

What you do

Distribute Information Sheet 23 to the students and discuss with them how advertisements with which they are familiar relate to these guidelines.

Ask the students to devise and then storyboard an advertisement for an alcoholic drink. If this is done in small groups then the final storyboards can be exchanged between the groups and analysed. How do the advertisements they have created set about selling their product? How do they compare with the guidelines on Information Sheet 23?

Notes

The discussion arising from this exercise can be widened to include representation of smoking, drinking or abusing drugs in media texts other than advertisements. This could be prompted by giving the students a list of genres, for example, and asking them to rank them in the order of texts most likely to contain such representations and extended to discuss how the audiences for texts belonging to such genres are addressed by these representations (e.g. the characters in *Platoon* smoke a lot, characters in soap operas tend to be shown drinking, etc.).

The British Code of Advertising Practice

Drink Advertising
(section C.X11)

1   Advertisements should be **socially responsible** and should not encourage excessive drinking. In particular, they should not exploit the young, the immature, or those with mental or social incapacities.

2.1   Advertisements should not be directed at **people under 18** whether by selection of the medium or context in which they appear, or by reason of their content or style of presentation.

2.2   No advertisement should feature any **characters**, real or fictitious, who are likely whether because of their apparent youth or otherwise, to attract the particular attention or admiration of people under 18 and thereby, in any way, to encourage them to drink.

2.3   People who are under 18 should not appear in advertisements except when their presence would be neither illegal nor unusual; for example, as participants in such events as **family celebrations**. When they are so shown, it should always be obvious that they are not drinking.

2.4   **People shown drinking** in advertisements should always clearly be adults; and to ensure that this is the impression created, advertisers should not engage as models people under 25, or people who look as though they may be under 25, if these people are to be shown in any advertisement either drinking or about to drive.

Tobacco Advertising
(Appendix 1)

Youth Rules (2.1, 4, 5, 11, 12, 13)

In interpreting the rules in relation to youth, advertisers should take special care not to address their advertisements particularly to young people, even where there is no suggestion that the products are for their consumption, e.g. where it is intended as a present for an adult. Thus people featured in cigarette advertisements should both be and clearly be seen to be adults 25 or over;

advertisements should not be designed, written or published in such a way as to make it likely that they will appeal more to those under 18 than to the public at large;

characters and situations depicted should not be such as to inspire the emulation of the young, by suggesting that those who do not smoke at all, or who do not smoke a particular brand are less grown up, less manly or less feminine than those who do, or that they are lacking in daring or sophistication.

(The Committee of Advertising Practice publish guidelines under the supervision of the Advertising Standards Authority.)

6   Morals and manners: 'bad' language

Background

The distinction between 'morals' and manners made by BBFC policy as formulated since 1975, has been touched upon in the earlier section on violence and obscenity legislation, when the idea of 'immoral' influence was outlined. This rationale for censorship is indicated in the duties and responsibilities laid at the door of free speech in Article 10 of the European Convention on Human Rights which, among other conditions, states that restrictions may be necessary on free speech 'for the prevention of disorder or crime and for the protection of health and morals'. The idea that people can be made 'morally bad' by films is one reason why censorship and classification of films and videos occurs and is distinct from earlier tests such as 'gross indecency', which depends on the shock and disgust of the notionally ordinary, decent 'man' rather than the idea that audiences can be offered pleasures which may increase the risk of crime through, for example, detailed representations of rape, or violence presented in such a way as to make vicarious sadism a main source of pleasure. These areas where the censor sees a possible harmful effect on public morality are also those areas where juries are likely to convict under the OPA. A great deal of regulatory activity concerns not this philosophically and politically debatable area of adult censorship deriving from moral welfare arguments, but simple offence at bad language in film, or nudity or other issues which can be grouped under the heading of 'manners'.

This area can be discussed with the class by talking about manners in real life. Students can discuss how they talk to each other, how they talk to their parents, etc. – whether different rules and codes apply to the way they or other people behave in real life in different circumstances. Concentrating on language, which is, in Britain, the main manners' issue, certainly when it comes to complaints to television stations, the teacher could ask why bad language is seen as more acceptable in some circumstances than others.

Would we be more likely to be shocked or affected by having someone swear casually in unusual circumstances – a doctor, for example, offering diagnosis to a patient – than hearing someone swear during an argument? On television, it would probably be more shocking – although it is so unlikely that it may also be funny – to hear the weather presenter swear while giving a weather report than hear characters in a play about football hooliganism do so, or, to use the extract for *Platoon* as an example, which uses a high number of words which could offend certain viewers.

It may be that people who are very offended by 'bad' language would argue that there is a moral component to this offence – that language is a centrally important part of human experience, and that the reduction of it to a handful of expletives is, in general terms, an immoral thing for a society to do. It could also be argued that swearing is one element in an overall impoverishment of language which leaves young people, if they are encouraged by film and videos to rely on expletives, disadvantaged in their range of vocabulary. The offence, however, if it is felt, is mostly one to the viewer's assessment of social propriety, rather than one which calls upon the strict definition of 'obscenity' in law; even an 'obscenity' remains an imprecise term often used to describe these individual words. John Trevelyan reveals the point at which it was clear that the use of 'sexual expletives' was no longer a matter for the courts:

> By 1970 the words 'fuck' and 'fucking' were accepted in 'X' films. It would have been difficult to resist this since they appeared in an increasing number of films. We were more reluctant to accept the word 'cunt' since this was generally regarded as more offensive. With the abandonment of the Lord Chamberlain's censorship of stage plays these words became common on the London stage, and presumably in provincial theatres also, and were in fairly frequent use in some newspapers and magazines. A judge in the United States and a London magistrate both ruled

that the words 'fuck' and 'fucking' could no longer be regarded as legally obscene. (Trevelyan, 1973, pp. 178-9.)

BBFC

The BBFC now deals with possible offence caused by language in films and videos by making language a consideration in the age classifications given to them. It is never cut from films in the adult category, but it is sometimes cut out of films at the distribution company's request to achieve lower categories. The question of language and offence has produced one of the very few sets of BBFC rules about the classification of films and videos: 'U' category material contains no swearing at all; 'PG' material can contain lavatorial swear words such as 'shit' and 'piss' and lower level 'bad' language of this variety; the strongest sexual expletives in terms of offence – 'fuck' and 'cunt' – in themselves demand a '15' or '18' certificate although an unobtrusive use of the former is allowed at '12'.

Social standards

The notion of 'society' which enforces classification and censorship decisions, constructs, in each country, a series of versions of national mores and standards out of a heterogeneous and widely varying sets of beliefs, standards and viewpoints. This is nowhere more clear than in the case of language, a subject which causes more complaints to media regulators in Britain than any other, and one which is not as high profile an issue in other, countries and for foreign classifiers, television stations, etc. Why should this be the case? As with many of the unresolvable issues raised in the classroom by this pack, the guesses of the pupils will be as valuable as anybody else's guess.

It could be that it is easier to cause offence through swearing in English than in other languages. English certainly has a wider range of words for this purpose than German or French – many French swear words have had their taboo elements removed over generations of usage. But this merely leads us back to the unanswerable question of why certain English words continue to carry such taboo power for many people in England, but arguably, for a comparatively small proportion of citizens of America or Australia. This cultural peculiarity is, of course, very visible in relation to films as most films released in Britain are American. The film and video censor's Annual Report for 1989 mentions this consideration and describes how 'bad' language was treated in films and videos submitted to the BBFC in that year:

Classification

> The perennial problem of bad language in American films is with us still, with classification the only tool when the distributor refuses to cut. Since UK film categories exclude those younger than the stated age, film companies are more inclined to cut the odd moment of bad language to secure the advisory 'PG' which helps the box office. Video companies rarely bother to cut, counting perhaps on the likelihood that parents will not be too strict with the viewing habits of younger teenagers, even when the label gives as the minimum age 15. In 1989, expletives were removed from six cinema films, in five cases to gain a 'PG' and in one to achieve a '12'. ... On video, twelve films were cut for 'PG' to remove expletives, and in one case adult sexual references, but it was often the Board which had to persuade the company to cut on the grounds that a certificate could not in all conscience be issued stating that the work is 'suitable only for persons of 15 years and over'. (Ferman, BBFC Annual Report, 1989 (1990), p. 12.)

(3,348 video features and 369 film features were submitted to the BBFC in 1989.)

The enduring nature of 'bad' language as an issue can be illustrated by its visibility in 1991, with regard to both video and television, in two areas:

- the frequency with which the video industry raised it as an issue in the trade press in that year; and
- the publication of two reports on 'bad' language and the media – one by Mary Whitehouse's pressure group, the National Viewers' and Listeners' Association, the second by the Broadcasting Standards Council.

The British Videogram Association (BVA), an industry body, one of whose concerns, via the Video Standards Council, is to maintain the 'image' of the video industry as a whole, believes that 'bad' language is a major source of public criticism of pre-recorded videotapes, a view the organisation bases on the reports of complaints from the public to video dealers. Information Sheet 24 (p.117) contains an article from a video trade journal *Video Trade Weekly* which reports on a poll commissioned by the video industry suggesting that 'bad' language was an issue and was used by the video industry to press for stricter classifications for language. The article again points to the connection between American standards, which have resulted in American distributors desiring the 'PG13' certificate and the occurrence of 'bad' language in videos. The class could be asked to question the implications of using age-related categories to minimise complaints in this way. Are fifteen- to seventeen-year-old viewers more or less likely to find certain language offensive? Are the complainants concerned at not being given enough information by the age-related category on the video sleeve? Or are they more concerned about allowing young people of fifteen to hear 'bad' language than about a film being classified '15' on video because of one use of one word? If the pupils have seen *Crocodile Dundee* on television, though, they will have seen a version that was already cut for transmission and which was without the offending word.

Language in the cinema is very rarely the subject of public complaints, but television companies receive a large number of letters about the subject. The NVLA report, entitled 'The Debasement of Language', also reported on a very small-scale survey conducted by the pressure group, which viewed a series of films after the nine o'clock watershed (which divides family viewing from adult viewing on television: twenty-nine films in 1989; thirty-seven in 1990 and sixteen at the beginning of 1991 (the four network television channels broadcast about thirty to forty feature films, mostly made for cinema but sometimes for American television every week). Monitoring the 'bad' language in these films, Mary Whitehouse's pressure group complained to the television stations that the incidence of swearing on television had increased. This move was part of a long-standing public campaign against swearing on television conducted by this group, and is worth discussing in that it does not address 'bad' language in children's programmes so much as suggest that bad language should be censored on late-night television for adults.

Broadcasting Standards Council

Towards the end of 1991, the Broadcasting Standards Council produced a report which surveyed 300 viewers and tested them with various words which viewers had complained about to measure their continued power to shock. Most people appeared to believe that there is too much swearing on television, but that several of the more taboo words, including the word 'fuck' are losing some of their capacity to cause offence. Swear words owing their taboo status to their affront to the Christian religion remained, unsurprisingly, taboo to those who described themselves as Christians, while one-half of those surveyed felt that words which owed their offensiveness to racial abuse should never be used in any context on television. The report points also to the significance of age and gender in the level of offence taken by 'bad' language – elderly women felt more offended by it than young men.

Activity 15 Classroom discussion on 'bad' language

Aim

- To encourage the students to think critically about why and how regulation of media texts must take account of social mores or manners.

Objective

- Students should be able to develop their own views on the issue of 'bad' language and the media informed by institutional and regulatory knowledge.

What you need

Information sheet 24 (p. 117) and Activity Sheet 10 (p. 118).

What you do

Distribute the sheets and use them as the basis for a classroom discussion. This could take the form of a debate for and against the motion that, for example, 'Any film to which people under twelve (or fifteen) have access should not contain any "bad" language', or '"Bad" language should not be a cause of regulation of media texts'. The debate could be designed as a Channel Four style *Right to Reply* simulation, using a Chair and producers talking to complainants on television. A specific time limit of 5 minutes could be imposed, as in the television programmes debate.

Notes

The passage on Activity Sheet 10 comes from Professor Phil Redmond's essay, *Class, Decency and Hypocrisy* published in the BSC's monograph on language. Redmond's experience as producer of *Grange Hill* and *Brookside* gave him firsthand experience of this issue.

This passage discusses the response to the first episodes of *Brookside* screened at the launch of Channel Four. Unlike other soap operas whose scripts attempt to be realistic without including swearing which might upset large audiences, *Brookside* began by having the characters talk exactly in the different ways the writer had observed real people talking in various social situations. This meant that a group of men depicted together in a pub would be more likely to swear than a family group at home, and the soap followed these realistic patterns and stayed true to its own internal contexts. The extract shows how this experiment proved that the most significant context of all for television is the viewing context, that the predominantly family audience for soap operas like *Brookside* did not want to hear 'bad' language irrespective of the fictitious context on screen.

© *Video Trade Weekly*
25 March 1991

Poll shows public 'concern' about swearing

The BVA and VSC push for tighter controls on *?!?*!*?*!!?! in videos

by Branwell Johnson

WHO GIVES a monkey's about bad language on video? Well, both the British Videogram Association and the Video Standards Council believe it is an issue of consumer concern.

Swearing on titles classified PG and 15 has been an industry topic for many years. However, to date, the trade bodies have had no strong statistical evidence that the public is concerned by bad language on video.

Now the BVA has results from a commissioned Gallup Poll showing about 49 per cent of those questioned hired a PG or 15 certificate title which contained language they felt required a stricter classification.

Iain Muspratt, BVA vice-chairman and vice-president of the VSC, said that the British Board of Film Classification felt the video industry was "oversensitive" about swearing. Armed with the new information, the trade bodies can now press for more discussion with the BBFC and the Video Consultative Council about swearing.

Muspratt said the BVA was not looking to establish a hard and fast list of what was and what was not permissible on video. "In general terms, we would like to see classification below 18 take proper account of the general disquiet which the public has in regard to bad language.

"We are looking for the BBFC to respond to public criticism," he said.

Laurie Hall, secretary general of the VSC, agreed that swearing was an issue, especially on PG titles. "We are really asking the question: Should a PG permit any swear words at all?"

He said the matter was bound up with the arguments for and against the introduction of the 12 certificate – officially opposed by the BVA – and believes words which now ensure a title a 15 certificate might find their way onto 12-classified titles.

Dealers who believe customers are sensitive to swearing include Peter Potter, of Dragon Videos in Anglesey, north Wales. He said customers commented on the bad language in RCA/Columbia's war drama *Platoon* (15), for instance. He added that he does make a point of telling customers about titles he knows contain heavy swearing.

Brian Eveleigh, of Stylers Video Centre in Somerset, said: "Most parents are a little bit upset that there is swearing on PG and 15 certificates, and most think there is no reason for it to be there."

Research on attitudes to bad language on television show it is a significant, but dwindling problem. The Independent Television Commission's annual survey, *Attitudes To Television In 1990*, shows swearing is still the main cause of offence on TV – but less people find it disturbing.

James Ferman, director of the BBFC, said films were occasionally given a stricter certificate on video than cinema due to language, citing CIC Video's *Harlem Nights* (up to 18 from 15) as an example.

He believed a 12 certificate would allow greater flexibility on handling language, but not open the floodgates, as very few swearwords were passed at 12 for cinema. He said he believed the BVA was "manufacturing an issue" in its battle against the 12 certificate.

Ferman added that the BBFC acted responsibly on language and responded to the message it received from the video industry. For example, it refused PG certificates to films containing sexual swearwords. *Crocodile Dundee* (FoxVideo) received a 15 due to one sexual swearword, but Ferman said the public was "dismayed at the [video] classification."

Both Ferman and Hall agreed that the Hollywood studios caused problems by insisting on the inclusion of swearwords to earn titles the commercially-advantageous PG-13 certificate in the US.

The PG-13 means a film is open to all, but suggests a title will be too strong for pre-teenagers – thereby encouraging them to see the film. Five titles in the US box office last year rated PG-13 had to be reclassified for video in the UK: *Gremlins 2 The New Batch* (Warner Home Video), *Ghost* (CIC), *Look Who's Talking* (20.20) and *Bird On A Wire* (CIC) were given a 15, while *Memphis Belle* (Warner) had swearing cut to make it a PG.

1. Why do you think swearing upsets people? Does it ever upset you? Either in real life or in films, videos or on television?
2. Which types of context do you think are important in deciding whether 'bad' language in a film or programme is going to upset members of the audience?
3. Read the extract by Phil Redmond below. In what ways, in the words of Phil Redmond, do television programmes 'cut across social mores'? Is the situation different with films and videos?
4. Do you think some viewers of videos are more likely to be upset by 'bad' language than if they were watching the same film in the cinema? Why?

Phil Redmond

It was with *Brookside* that I found myself totally out of step with the audience. In 1982, I wanted, as a writer and producer, to challenge the almost ridiculous notion of one combination of letters upsetting people more than another combination. In 1982 I felt it was time to face this taboo – it was, after all, the 1980s.

So on 2nd November 1982 to an unsuspecting public, *Brookside* was launched on Channel Four. The public were unsuspecting because the press, to that date, had been full of comparisons with *Coronation Street.* Although the intent was to create the first 'soap-war' – a term only created in later years when *EastEnders* emerged – the result was that the nation was expecting 'Sons and Daughters of Coronation Street'. Pleasingly enough, 4.2 million tuned in to the first episode – and the tabloids went berserk the next day with their 'Channel Swore' headlines …

Still my real lesson came from the really intelligent people – the audience – as I witnessed an extremely effective demonstration of an oft denied cliché – 'if they don't like it, they'll switch off'. And they did. From 2nd November 1982 until July 1983 *Brookside's* audience dropped from 4.2 million to approximately 500,000.

From the letters, conversations and discussions I had, it was clear that the audience did not like the swearing – especially at 5.00 p.m. on a Saturday afternoon. Although viewers understood that we were following all society's accepted social mores – men swearing on the factory floor, but not at home; kids swearing between themselves, but not in front of teachers or parents, etc. – they just did not like it. Why? Because the programme itself could cut across these social mores. Families would view together. Men, women, adults, children. They could not enforce the social mores. They were not in control of their social behaviour.

(Andrea Millwood Hargrave (ed.), *A Matter of Manners? The Limits of Broadcast Language,* London, John Libbey/ BSC, 1991.)

When it comes to video and the different television carrying systems the situation is very different. A video recorder and monitor can be set up anywhere and is often under the control of the viewer when it comes to time of viewing and viewing situations. (Happily, choosing to view films in empty cinemas is not the option it used to be before the revival of cinema's fortunes.) New developments in technology could also give those fortunate enough to be able to afford the equipment the opportunity to sit in a cinema or watch a video on a miniature television and 8mm video 'Watchman' if the film becomes boring. The Video Recordings Act, though, defines video as primarily a domestic medium – it is 'home video' to which the Act refers. The Act also defines 'home' as a place where children are likely to be present and potentially exposed to unsuitable video images. It is only a minority of homes, however, which have children as part of the household. The association of home with children has been one of the reasons why video has been treated more strictly by the regulators than film. It has not meant, as many critics feared in the mid-80s, that all videos have been reduced to 'PG' levels. But, the presence of children apart for a moment, video does not have to be seen as a domestic medium. It could be used by groups of citizens to make and show their own videos to other members of the community in communal situations: political meetings, for example. It can be used, of course, in education.

With mass production of video camcorders, it is possible for individuals and groups to produce audiovisual material themselves, thus challenging in some small way the most significant aspect of censorship in the media: the fact that only a tiny minority of citizens have, during the century in which the audiovisual media developed as a system of mass communication, had access to the means of producing such communications. On a more mundane level, video can be used instead of film projection in cinemas, something which has already been introduced in the smaller auditoria of some regional multiplexes. Video could also be used in public spaces – this is a prevalent motif in such science fiction films

as *Blade Runner* (US, Ridley Scott, 1982) and *Total Recall* (US, Paul Verhoeven, 1990), and is already present in advertising videos screened in department stores and to convey images of musical performers to large open-air crowds, many of whom are too far away to see the stage.

The main reason for video being conceived of as home entertainment is that video hardware was developed in the 70s and 80s as a domestic consumer product. Videotape recording has been in existence since 1951 when Bing Crosby's entertainment company commissioned the electronics firm Ampex to produce a videotape recorder after they had successfully developed a reel-to-reel audiotape recorder in the 40s so the singer could record his high-rating radio show. It was used in the production of television programmes in the 50s and 60s but developed as a consumer item by analogy with television sets in the 70s. The hardware itself was marketed as a desirable item independent of the available software in the late 70s and early 80s, and systems which did place the emphasis on collectable software – such as the Laserdisc player (which found a market only when shorn of images in the software-orientated audio sector as the CD) – were less successful than when there was the hardware with the capacity to record.

The emergence of the hardware before the systematic production of software meant that before 1983, and the appearance of the video industry's copyright investigation and enforcement body FACT (Federation Against Copyright Theft), all films released on video in Britain were pirate copies taken from film prints. According to Gunter more than half the homes in Britain with a television also had a video recorder and 69 per cent of family households with children had video recorders. In discussing why video can be seen predominantly as a transmission and distribution system aimed at the private home, students could also be directed towards the functioning of copyright law in this respect. Below, for example, is the copyright warning which appears at the start of pre-recorded videotapes distributed by Columbia Tri-Star Home Video:

Pupils could be asked to consider whether copyright restrictions like this are a form of economic regulation and self-protection, which can be seen as a form of censorship affecting the direction in which technological media develop.

Video, again, does not have a one-to-one relationship to the viewing situations listed in C (Activity Sheet 11). With cinema, for example, 'viewing with strangers' is nearly always the case while 'viewing alone' is hardly ever the case. With video all these viewing situations could occur. Hence the questionnaires employed in the first section of this workbook could be referred to. A useful comparison with the results of these is provided by a survey conducted by Barrie Gunther and Mark R. Levy (in Gunther, Barrie and Mallory, Usher, *The Uses and Impact of Home Video in Great Britain*, 1989, pp. 50-69.) into the social contexts of video viewing. These researchers drew a distinction between broadcast television watched off-air and playback of television programmes which had been recorded. A sample of VCR owners in a family context filled in viewing diaries and answered questions about the usual situations in which they watched videos. 74 per cent of those taking part said that it was a family occasion, 40 per cent said it was an enjoyable way to spend time with friends. These statements did not correspond to the evidence of the viewing diaries, which suggested that 59 per cent of videos are played back by adults alone and a further 22 per cent with an adult from the same household. Only 12 per cent were viewed with children or a mixture of adults and children from the same household. Does this suggest that despite going into the family situation that video may be a different way of viewing audiovisual material than television? Is this due to the deliberate individual choice involved in (1) hiring or purchasing a cassette or (2) deciding to copy something from broadcast or other forms of television to be viewed later? If this is true, does it make sense that broadcast television, which may be more likely to be viewed in a family context should be more strictly regulated than video, as indeed it is, (particularly with regard to manners' issues like language discussed in the last section)?

The pupils should be directed towards extending this discussion to the other connections they have made between the three lists. What does this observation about the relationship involved lead them to think about the way the medium is likely to be regulated? Does this accord with their own experience? To focus this a bit more it is proposed now to offer a striking example of the link between viewing context and regulation.

A Transmission/distribution system

- cinema
- broadcast television
- satellite television
- cable television
- still photography
- video
- computers

B Viewing locations

- theatres
- the home
- the workplace
- transport
- the street and other public places

C Viewing situations

- alone
- with family
- with friends
- with strangers

Select combinations of at least one from A, B and C. Discuss what different possibilities there are for you. For example, do you usually watch satellite television (A) at home, (B) with your family, or (C) alone? Which are the systems listed in A which allow for the most viewing situation and locations? Do you think definitions sometimes overlap? Are films shown on television, for example, best seen as television or cinema?

Activity 17 Simulation

Aim

- To understand conceptual issues relating to audience reception and consumption.

Objective

- Students should be able to investigate how viewing contexts may affect regulation/programming of media texts.

What you need
Activity Sheet 12 (p. 125).

What you do
Distribute the sheet to the students. Instruct the students in groups to consider either question 1 or 2.

Notes
Films shown on international transport, on aeroplanes (or ships) are not viewed separately by the BBFC in the light of the specific viewing contexts involved. Most of them do have certificates from the classification body of the airline's home country, but these are the ones given to the film for theatrical distribution in cinemas. The version of the film the passengers will see, if the original film has been given anything other than a 'U' or 'PG' certificate, is, though, unlikely to be the one viewers would have seen in the cinema. The airlines employ In-flight Entertainment Managers who are responsible for the provision of suitably distracting entertainment for passengers, a job which has existed since 1961 when the first in-flight film was screened on an aeroplane using 16mm film. Over ninety airlines now offer films during long flights and a large number of these use video projection equipment. Often the large American companies which provide the equipment also provide the film

programmes as well. Airlines are concerned, however, that a trapped audience of sometimes anxious passengers are not presented with anything likely to disturb it. Surprisingly, many Hollywood films fall into this category in this viewing context.

In an article on the regulation of in-flight films, Rosemary Stark has pointed out the way the specific profile of an audience comprising airline passengers affects the choice of film and whether it is censored. The factors are:

- The average age of the airline passenger is between forty and forty-two-years-old. The 'normal' cinemagoer addressed by Hollywood films is generally eighteen to twenty-five.
- The audience is likely to include young children.
- The airline passengers are by definition from different national backgrounds and sometimes bring different cultural values to bear on the films.
- This audience may include passengers who are nervous about flying.

The third point would make an interesting topic for discussion in the classroom. Would the *Rambo* films, for example, be suitable viewing on flight to South East Asia? What about films emphasising the consumption of alcohol on flights to Middle East countries where alcohol is banned? Films with many images of violence – the *Dirty Harry* films for example – tend to be banned by Scandinavian censor boards; based on assessment of community standards in these countries which are tolerant towards depictions of sex but not violence, so this type of film tends not to be shown on flights to these countries. The fourth point explains why disaster movies are not shown on airlines.

In practice, films are heavily censored, as Rosemary Stark points out:

> When you fly between countries, censorship becomes a much more sensitive issue. It must tackle not just the conventional decency-offending areas of sex,

violence, nudity and bad language, but also address itself to particular political sensibilities; and of course to the circumstances in which the movie will be shown, with passengers of all ages strapped into their seats having had no prior say in the choice of their entertainment or the company with which they would choose to share it. A film you might have enjoyed with your spouse can turn into an experience of sweaty embarrassment with your child or grandmother sitting beside you, undistractably agog or tutting with outrage. (Stark, (Moving Pictures), Signature, pp. 16-17.)

Films are cut for this audience to remove a range of material, either by the video hardware corporations supplying the equipment, or as is increasingly the case, American studios offer different versions which have been assembled in the post-production stage of film-making, often using 'cover material' – that is, material which is shot at the same time as the footage used to construct the final film but which may employ different camera angles to remove nudity, for example. This 'airline version' as it is known, has other uses – it often appears on American television and sometimes on British television as a 'television version'.

Viewing Contexts

1. You are the In-flight Entertainment Manager of Edison Airlines and the chief executive of the airline asks you to consider the future of entertainment on Edison aircraft. The choices are:

   - improving the video projection system to give better sound and picture quality so that everybody in the aeroplane could see the same screen;
   - introduce a new satellite link up delivering Edison Vision, a mix of programmes and films, to all aircraft simultaneously regardless of their destination;
   - introduce individual monitors in the seat backs with a choice of films and programmes. (Monitors would unavoidably be visible to passengers in neighbouring seats.)

   Discuss these alternatives bearing in mind that your job requires you to provide passengers with distracting entertainment without causing complaints about the contents of this entertainment.

2. While you still have the video projection system you have the choice of the following films to show in a flight from New York to Hanoi. Which films would you choose and why, bearing in mind the considerations mentioned in 1 above.

   - *Top Gun* ('PG')
   - *Platoon* ('15')
   - *Airport* ('PG')
   - *Nightmare on Elm Street* ('18')
   - *The Addams Family* ('PG')
   - *Terminator 2* ('15')

(If you are unfamiliar with any of these films, look them up in a film guide.)

8   Censorship, the press and publicity

Introduction
This section aims to introduce classroom discussion and activity on the relationship between the press and the regulation of film, video and television. It is not concerned with regulation and censorship of the press – teaching this would have, among other things, to include a look at the work of regulatory bodies like the Press Complaints Commission, studies of patterns of ownership and case studies on, for example, the reporting of the Gulf War in 1991. This section is primarily concerned with the way the press may be felt to set an agenda for censorship and regulation by:

• the reviewing of films;
• the reporting of controversy surrounding films and videos;
• the reporting of crime.

In working on these areas, pupils will be asked to think about the links between the activities listed above and publicity and advertising for films. The workbook concludes with information and activities on the way this latter area has been subject to self-regulation by the video industry.

Activity 18   Criticism and reviewing

Aim

• To understand how ideas and 'debates' about morality and regulation are circulated in publicity and press media.

Objective

• Students should be able to investigate the relationship between press reviews and regulation.

What you need
Information Sheets 25 and 26 (pp. 129 and 130).

What you do
Distribute the information sheets and use these as the basis for a class discussion. Ask the students to talk about whether they read film reviews before going to the cinema, or read reviews, film guides, etc. when watching films on video or on television. What purposes do they think film reviews serve? Are there different types of review for different types of journal and newspaper? Depending on the time available, pupils could collect and discuss different types of review – from film journals like *Sight and Sound,* to reviews in different newspapers, from the tabloids to the 'qualities'.

Notes
In order to focus this discussion, a question can be posed about what some of the press reviews of *The Wild One* and the censor's decision to ban it have in common. They tend to be based on judgments on the conditions of the day, even if the principle underlying these judgments seems to remain constant. The students could consider the extracts from film reviews of two films with which they may be familiar (see Information Sheet 25). The film titles have been omitted

so students can focus on the content of the comment without prejudging it. The first is from a review of *The Godfather* (US, Francis Ford Coppola, 1971) and the second is referring to *Psycho* (US, Alfred Hitchcock, 1960). These are two quite extreme examples of the way in which severe moral judgments about films tend to wear rather less well than the films themselves. With these two films controversy was a large element in the publicity and information surrounding their release, an element which is now invisible when they are seen on television – *The Godfather* was cut for its initial release in 1972 although the '18'-certificated video version is uncut and the film has been transmitted in this form on the BBC. (It had previously been shown in a 'TV' version which had the 'bad' language edited out.) *Psycho* was passed '15' on video in 1988 in an uncut version, the famous shower sequence having now become the subject of endless parodies and pastiches in other films and also in television commercials and comedy sketches. Below is John Trevelyan's outline of his response to *Psycho* when it was submitted to the BBFC in 1960:

> Hitchcock's *Psycho* ... included a sadistic killing of a naked girl in a shower. The girl was stabbed fourteen times and we had shots of blood all over the place, fortunately in black and white and not in colour. I told Hitchcock that we would have to cut this scene, not only because it was sadistic but because recently there had been much publicity in the press on two sensational killings, one in which a girl student had been decapitated. The scene was cleverly shot and edited like a jigsaw puzzle, but we were able to reduce the stabbing to three or four strokes and thus, to some extent to lessen the sadism. (Trevelyan, 1977, p. 100.)

Film reviews are the public's main source of information, along with publicity produced by distribution companies about the nature and content of films. One function is therefore to warn people about the type of film they might not want to see. One role of the critic and reviewer is therefore to give personal opinions which function as consumer advice and many newspaper reader's view of the cinema is probably shaped by the likelihood that they have read more reviews than they have seen films. Often, also, film reviews address readers who do not go to the cinema but who are curious about what is on release.

In the past, although film critics have openly campaigned against representations of violence in films (*Straw Dogs* and *Clockwork Orange* are described in Part Two p. 20), and most would probably express ambivalence about censorship, can some film criticism also contribute to a climate in which calls for more censorship of films are likely to be raised? Activity Sheet 26 (p. 136) reproduces a piece by Barry Norman describing a film which was passed '18' without cuts by the BBFC, which can be discussed in this light.

Films, videos and television being the most popular forms of mass entertainment, constitute irresistible topics for the popular press. Press material collected by pupils can be assessed and compared for their perspectives on those issues considered important by regulators. Do the reviews predispose readers to conclude that greater or lesser regulation should take place?

It is mostly the case that by the time films are previewed for the press, they have already been classified by the BBFC, although American films often arrive after their release in the US has generated publicity – *Cape Fear* (US, Martin Scorsese, 1991) is an example of this, although the publicity did not directly affect the film's classification. The increasing concern with which the BBFC viewed the *Rambo* films, which led to *Rambo III* (US, Peter MacDonald, 1988) being cut for the '15' certificate, can be seen alongside increasing interest on the press's part in linking *Rambo* to criminals who had adopted survivalist pursuits modelled on those in the film. The cuts were mostly to images glamorising Rambo's commando knife, which was appearing increasingly in courts as a dangerous weapon.

Censorship, the press and publicity

BRANDO'S FILM SCREAMS A HYMN TO THE GLORY OF VIOLENCE

– Being released here with a 'X' certificate all over the country, including four cinemas in London, is the religion for all who believe in life for life, eye for eye. It is the sort of movie that gives easy conscience to an IRA gunman, dignity to the Kray twins and hope to drug pedlars and bent cops.
– Never since Goebbels has the propaganda of violence been so beautifully put together. Yet thanks to its bizarre publicity and the hysterical acclaim of the American public (already the film has busted the *Gone With the Wind* gross takings) critical appraisal of it is totally superfluous. You are going to see it no matter what.

(*The Sun,* 22 August, 1972)

MURDER WHILE YOU WATCH

There is a certain fascism of the spirit, which in non-Fascist countries expresses itself in films like this. It is the businesslike Kraft-Ebbing equivalent of Leni Riefenstahl's pre-war propaganda film, *Triumph of the Will,* a coupling of naked sado-sexual exhibitionism with a profound awareness of the techniques most liable to hold an audience by its viscera, which leaves me less disgusted than frightened for the man who made the picture and the people who will like it. There is not an ounce of decency, or of genuine human artistry evident in front of or behind the cameras: the thing is calibrated to exploit our most secret and hostile sexual fantasies ... this is more miserable than the most miserable peep show I have ever seen, far more awful and suggestive than the most pornographic film I have seen. And for the record, as a produced story it is uninteresting.

(Clancy Sigal, *Time & Tide,* 20 August, 1960)

Taking violence into a new dimension

BARRY NORMAN

SCREEN SCENE

Perhaps the time has come to re-evaluate the contribution of special effects to contemporary cinema. Of all modern technological advances in the movies – better cameras, faster film and the like – that of special effects (or FX as they're known in the trade) has been quite the most dramatic.

Unfortunately, that's not entirely good news. On the credit side, FX have certainly added credibility to space epics – the opening shot of 'Star Wars', for example, when the space ship seems to be flying directly over your head.

A shot like that would have been virtually impossible before 1977 when the film was made and it was greeted with understandable admiration and excitement.

On the debit side, however, the success and influence of 'Star Wars' was such that for a number of years it led to a spate of imitations, lesser movies by lesser directors than George Lucas, in which the technology was more important than the characters or the plot.

The constant complaint during that period was that films were no longer about people – they were about machinery.

This is not longer quite so true. The cinema's infatuation with space age tales has dimmed a little of late but the influence of FX has not. Now they are dominating other genres, in particular the thriller and the horror film.

And their use in one particular current picture leads me to the uneasy belief that FX are largely responsible for the excessive amount of violence in films today.

The example I have in mind is 'Robocop', a futuristic story about a cop who, having been shot and left for dead, is turned into a cyborg – half man, half robot – and sent out to blast crime of the streets.

In parts it's a witty, imaginative and entertaining movie, almost a very good one indeed, except for a degree of violence that I found sickening.

And I suspect that, after years of professional film watching I'm thinking of the scene in which the cop is cornered by a psychotic gang and shot to pieces and I mean that literally. Under a hail of bullets he has both legs and one arm shot off.

The scene is grotesquely and unnecessarily long and graphic and I have an idea it's there only because the film-makers were carried away by the FX.

It's easy to imagine them standing around in growing excitement as the boffins got to work. 'Gee, can you believe this? I mean, it's like you can actually see his legs coming off! And his arm! And, boy, look at the bullets going into his chest and his head – man, you can see them going in! There's no way we can leave this out of the movie, it's gotta go in!'

And in it went, taking screen violence into a new dimension of sadism and turning the audience, whether it likes it or not, into so many voyeurs. In the process that, and similar scenes, ruined the picture. My fear is that as FX gets even better, 'Robocop' could turn out to be a forerunner of even worse things to come.

Activity 19 Controversy and the press

Aim

- To highlight the interrelationship between the circulation of secondary texts with film and video texts.

Objective

- Students should be able to investigate how the press links controversy and film and video texts.

What you need

Information Sheets 27-31 (pp. 135-139). You could also ask the students to gather press material which links video and film with real-life issues such as crime.

What you do

Distribute the sheets and use them as a basis for a classroom discussion of the links between the press, publicity and the existence of censorship. A debate could focus on the motion that 'if newspapers reported a crime, film and video responsibly there would be less censorship of these media'. The debate could be simulated from different viewpoints: students could attempt to 'represent' The National Viewers' and Listeners' Association (Mary Whitehouse), Exhibitors, etc.

Notes

The Rambo phenomenon is productive in itself because it reveals the confused messages that the public are often offered by newspapers when they deal with films and controversy. The same newspaper which links real-life criminals to films by describing them as 'Rambo Killers' in its headlines one week will be availing itself of the ability of Hollywood films to sell copies of newspapers by running Rambo lookalike contests. Information Sheet 27 (p. 135) reproduces an article which points to the tabloid press's general use of and contribution to publicity generated by a film. This article is about the problem of young men taking drugs to produce muscular physiques.

This is a separate type of journalism from that dealing with the idea of links between representations of violence in films and awful real-life crime. This latter form of journalism can, of course, be motivated by genuine concern about the issue. However polemically expressed, the *Daily Mail* article reproduced in Information Sheet 31 (p. 139), had some connection with the real fears of its readers, and amidst the 'moral panic' over video nasties in 1984 there were some measured press articles – particularly the *Guardian*'s 'Where Do You Draw the Line?' series – which addressed these issues responsibly. Appendix II also mentions some of the serious research which has gone into attempts to isolate links between representations of violence and violence in real life.

However, the idea of a direct connection between popular film fiction and real crime is also a means by which real crime can be fictionalised and trivialised. The line between fantasy and reality can be crossed in the tabloids' predilection for seeing everything in terms of media fictions – whether by treating soap-opera characters as if they were real people or, as in the piece reproduced for classroom discussion on Information Sheet 28 (p. 136), as though real crimes were directly caused by films. Two of the videos referred to in this article have been banned by the BBFC – *I Spit on Your Grave* and *Last House on the Left* – and it would be inadvisable to focus too much discussion on these, as it should not be an outcome of work on censorship in school that pupils' curiosities about rejected films be aroused. (It is for the stated reason of not arousing interest in adults that the BBFC's Annual Reports do not refer to the titles of rejected videos.) The pupils may be familiar with some of the other titles. *The Thing* (US, John Carpenter, 1982) is a science fiction horror film with extravagant monster effects, which was passed '18' uncut on video and shown with a small edit for 'bad' language on network television.

Jagged Edge (US, Richard Marquand, 1985) and *Fatal Attraction* (US, Adrian Lyne, 1987) have both been screened on television in cut versions, and were both passed '18' on video. *Rambo: First Blood, Part II* (US, George Pan Cosmatos, 1985) was passed '15' uncut on video. The peculiarity of including the film *Fuzz* (US, Richard Colla, 1972) starring Racquel Welch and based on one of the '87th Precinct' novels of crime writer Ed McBain, which are very much like the television series *Hill Street Blues,* is indicated by the review of the film by the American showbusiness magazine *Variety* at the time of the film's release:

> The assorted people involved innocently or criminally with the police are neither patronized middle class or anointed low life. There is compassion in the treatment of all the characters, while at the same time their foibles are milked for both laughs and occasionally chilling reality. (24.5.1972, p. 19).

The press extract on Information Sheet 29 (p. 137) is from a local newspaper report on the arrest of a young man who had made a glove similar to that constructed and worn by the famous supernatural character Freddy Krueger in the *Nightmare on Elm Street* films. When the BBFC viewed the first of this series (US, Wes Craven, 1984) there was much discussion in the organisation on the imitability of the villain's trademark 'claws'. It was concluded that this was unlikely to be adopted as a weapon as, in contrast to novel weapons in martial arts films, for example, it is not being shown in the film as an efficient violent tool to be admired but in order to scare the audience – it also rather resembles the long fingernails of a witch and therefore connects Freddy with other traditional monster figures. Does this piece of journalism have anything in common with the 'Video Chiller' article? How effective is this as (i) reporting the facts and (ii) publicity, incidental or otherwise for a film? Would it make any difference, for example, if the piece had added that the party this young man was on his way to was a fancy dress party? Here, it is clear also that the irresponsibility of walking around in public with knives should be stressed by the teacher.

Finally, a brief look at the way the press can set an agenda for the discussion of censorship could include a look at how polemics on video and violence in the press can affect or reflect how people think about the media as a whole. Information Sheet 30 (p. 138) reproduces a column that appeared in a daily newspaper arguing strongly against the perceived 'evils' of video, and which caused the video industry itself to reply. This may be used by the teacher as the basis of work on how discussions on these issues often have practical, economic, social and legal components. The original article is a polemic in favour of stricter legislation. The reply is concerned with protecting the image of the industry. This letter concerns us, as we have seen, and is of central importance in the ongoing establishment of film censorship in 1913.

Self-regulation and publicity
This workbook concludes with an attempt to focus classroom discussion on the idea of self-regulation. This idea is often proposed as:

- an alternative to censorship imposed by outside bodies like the BBFC, ASS, ITC, etc.;
- one result of the existence of regulation;
- the most effective form of regulation, whereby the individual, armed with information and discretion decides what is suitable for him or herself and younger members of their family group.

Self-regulation by industries
The BBFC can be thought of as an industry self-regulatory body as its funding derives from viewing fees paid by distributors for classification of their films and videos. Its powers of classification and censorship are, however, underpinned by law, either through the requirement that

cinemas be licensed or through the Video Recordings Act. Similarly, the United States' Motion Pictures Code of 1930, mentioned in Section 3, was a piece of self-regulation which only became effective when 'seal of approval' began to have economic consequence for the distribution of films. Today, films are sometimes cut by American distributors to achieve the MPAA's 'R' certificate and avoid the limited distribution enforced by the prohibitive category 'NC17'. A more contentious form of industry self-regulation was presented by the 'Hollywood Blacklist' of the 50s, when the Hollywood film industry, under pressure from right-wing politicians, attempted to purge itself of so-called political 'radicals' among writers and directors. The class will also have been invited to think about the censorship involved in the way expensive Hollywood films have a strong interest in not alienating mass audiences so as to recoup their large budgets.

Hollywood films which run the risk of upsetting large numbers of the potential audience are rare, and these often cause headlines. Martin Scorsese's *The Last Temptation of Christ* (US/Canada, 1988), for example, was passed '18' on film and video but remains untransmitted on television due to the television company's fears about upsetting some viewers. Some of the case studies discussed earlier can be reconsidered in this light. In what ways do these films 'censor themselves' by considering what would be acceptable and unacceptable to sections of the audience? The students could be reminded of *The Wild One's* attempt to put both sides of the youth-versus-age theme it raises. Students could be prompted to seek out other examples of this.

Another example of self-regulation already touched upon is the way the film industry in the United States reacted to the claims that its films were 'selling drugs to children'. An example, closer to home, of a self-regulatory system are the arrangements for vetting the advertisement and sleeve packaging of videocassettes. The Video Packaging Review Committee logo may not have been noticed by pupils, but it now appears on the back of video sleeves along with the video distributor's logo, the name of the copyright holders of the contents of the video and of the artwork on the packaging and the video classification symbol. The VPRC is a arrangement between the British Videogram Association, the BBFC and the Advertising Standards Authority which was instituted in 1987.

The appearance of lurid video packaging in the high street in the early 80s was one way in which worries from different quarters about the contents of videos led to the 'video nasties' campaign. Video packaging is, of course, designed to sell videos. It achieves this by providing a 'narrative image' of the film, the posing of questions to the audience – through offering a series of images which give partial information and ideas about the nature of the film, ideas which can be only be drawn together as a whole when one sees the film. (Ellis, 1982, pp. 30-35). Pupils could be asked to bring in video sleeves and discuss how the sleeves are attempting to sell the film contained in the video – what it tells them about the narrative and more particularly the pleasures that the video may offer.

Regulating the appearance of video sleeves is concerned with the overall image of the video industry in the eyes of a large public, and is motivated by clear pragmatic aims. Video sleeves are an open display to children of any age, and so parents can easily be disturbed by the idea of gruesome images appearing on them. Although this is also the case with books in bookshops, the publishing industry has less reason to be concerned with its image than the more recent video industry whose arrival was marked by public moral outrage.

The VPRC comprises rotating representatives of the Advertising Standards Authority who consider whether to give the seal of approval to the finished sleeve. Without this vetting the BBFC will not issue a certificate, which means, in turn, that the video cannot be released. This, then, is a form of industry self-regulation which is at one remove backed by the statutory force of the Video Recordings Act. In February 1994, the video games industry created a self-regulatory film category coding system to allow parents and children to classify the suitability of video games.

Postscript

The information and exercises in this pack on the topic of classification and censorship have aimed at providing the pupils with a grasp of how regulatory media institutions work and the kind of considerations they bring to bear on making decisions about what the public, and, in particular, young people should see. What makes the area of censorship and regulation difficult to discuss and teach is that it rests on lines being drawn by institutions in the face of competing pressures from different and often irreconcilable sources, such as the industry, the press, pressure groups, etc. How films, videos and video games should be regulated is no more subject to a national overall consensus than other questions in the media – such as which films deserve distribution or transmission, or indeed, which films deserve to be funded in the first place.

The industrial processes which produce films and videos create conflicts and compromise. Where a measure of freedom is to be found, though, is with the viewer, who can choose between the various end results of these processes: to use the on/off button on the television, make their views felt about media products and exercise informed and discriminating choice. In the end it is education in all its forms, including media education, which can produce more democratic and responsible media practice and use rather than censorship, and it is to be hoped that teaching specifically about censorship has contributed in some small way to this process.

© *The Mail on Sunday,*
15 December 1985

The Mail on Sunday, December 15, 1985

FITNESS FANS LURED BY DANGER DRUGS

The deadly craze to look just like Rambo

MICHAEL is 19, unemployed and, with a lot of his council estate friends, has taken up the latest craze — body-building.

Forget sniffing glue: this year every youth on the street is pumping iron in a bid to look like Rambo.

And in seedy gyms, even by mail order, the kids are buying lethal drugs to help them.

The Mail on Sunday has uncovered a vast black market in steroids — synthetic hormones that can cause heart failure, cancer, liver damage, sterility and aggressive mental disorders.

Olympic

Unscrupulous dealers are cashing in. This week we bought three boxes of steroids from an unassuming business woman in Leicester. She told us there was a 20 per cent discount for orders over £100.

The sale of steroids is illegal and our file on the black market dealers has been handed to the authorities.

Michael, from Lewisham,

Special Investigation
By GRAEME GOURLAY

South London, bought a pack of Proviron steroids for £10 from a friend.

'I got into body-building about a year ago. It's a good hit, you feel good and look good.

'Well, this guy offers me some steroids. I thought "Why not? They can't be that dangerous with all them Olympic athletes taking them".

'Then after about six or seven weeks I started to feel strange. I kept getting into fights and things. Then I went off sex.'

'I got scared. I didn't feel right so I flushed them down the toilet.'

Kevin, a 26-year-old builder from Nottingham, started entering body-building competitions this year and began taking steroids. 'I didn't like it, but you've got no choice,' he said.

This summer he took a course, and in a month put on a stone — mostly muscle. By next year he expects to be

taking 250mg injections once a week.

'What worries me is the kids who end up taking vast doses', says Kevin.

'They think if one pill a day makes you put on so much muscle then ten pills will put on ten times as much.'

Price

Kevin bought his current supply of steroids through a classified advertisement in Bodybuilding Monthly.

We traced the advertiser, Advanced Sports, to a well-kept modern council flat in Leicester. The business is run by a woman calling herself Margaret Claxton, but the name on the electoral roll is McGrath.

When our investigator told her he was interested in steroids she gave him a price list and said most of the drugs were available. She sold him £27 worth. Steroids are not a controlled drug like

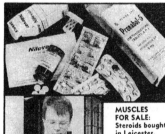

MUSCLES FOR SALE: Steroids bought in Leicester, . . . or Marbella

heroin, but selling them is illegal without a prescription.

People can legally import them for private use and this summer thousands of youths flocked to chemists in Spanish holiday resorts. Last week reporter Nigel Bowden was

easily able to buy steroids on the Costa del Sol. Chemists in Fuengirola and Marbella said they sold large quantities to young foreigners.

Jail

In Madrid a government spokesman at first said that it was strictly illegal to sell steroids without a prescription.

When we showed him the packets we had bought he said: 'There must be some mistake. Maybe they were old stock.'

In England the black market is now so big steroids are stolen. Earlier this year Newcastle gym-owner Ron Lowes was jailed for receiving 75,000 steroid tablets. The court heard that he sold them for £10 per 100.

Yesterday Lowes — who was released from prison last month — said: 'There are much worse things in the world. You would be better getting rid of cigarettes.

'The best way to end the black market in this country would be to make them legal. It's like everything else — if you want it you go out and get it.'

© *The Sun*
2 May 1990

THE VIDEO CHILLERS UNLEASHING MAD KILLERS

I HEARD VOICE OF VIDEO MICHAEL

From yesterday's Sun

WHEN Robert Sartin went on his gun rampage through the streets of his quiet town, he claimed he was driven by a voice from a video. He told a court that he had become obsessed with Michael Myers—the chilling central character in the Halloween movies. There have been several macabre episodes in which people claim they have been driven to evil by the exploits of video madmen. SUE CARROLL and ALLAN HALL investigate the video chillers.

JAGGED EDGE

● STUDENT Mark Branch, 18, had video parties with his pals, eating popcorn while blood splashed in buckets across the TV screen. Then he tried it for real, stabbing an 18-year-old girl with a long-bladed hunting knife and mutilating her body.

He hanged himself four days after the 1967 murder in Greenfield, Connecticut. Police Captain David Crossland said the killing was similar to the opening scenes of the Jeff Bridges horror film Jagged Edge.

BRIDGES: Killing

RAMBO

● BRIAN BRITTON worshipped the Rambo films so deeply, he thought he WAS Rambo.

Britton, 16, saw the Sly Stallone character as a way out of his real-life quarrels with his family and on March 22, 1989, toting two pump-action shotguns, he executed his father Dennis, 44, mother Marlene, 42, and brother James, eight.

When police surrounded the New York house and asked his name he yelled back, "Rambo."

SLY: Influence

I SPIT ON YOUR GRAVE

● PENSIONER Dick Slater wept as his son Ian was detained for life for causing grievous bodily harm to a ten-year-old girl and attempting to rape her.

Mr. Slater and his wife Barbara let their son watch films of sex and violence like the notorious I Spit On Your Grave because they believed it was part of growing up.

In this particular video nasty three gang rapes are featured, and the woman victim takes revenge. Each man is killed in a unique manner. One is seduced and castrated in the bath.

Dick, from Blackburn, Lancs, said later: "I thought he just treated them as a laugh."

FATAL ATTRACTION

● RONALD LEE, 29, brooded for a year about what to do to get back at his lover Mybrit Schaller, 26, who had dumped him for another boyfriend. He found his answer after seeing the film Fatal Attraction.

Lee went to her home in New Jersey with his semi-automatic rifle, and blasted her to death as she hugged new boyfriend Gerald McCord in front of the TV.

Then he turned the rifle on himself.

FATAL: Blasted

CRIMES OF PASSION

● EIGHTEEN-year-old Robin Gecht was a ticking time-bomb of frustrated emotions who blew up after he watched the Ken Russell film Crimes Of Passion, about a priest who terrorises a prostitute.

Satan-worshipper Gecht left his Chicago home after seeing the movie, which stars Kathleen Turner. He stalked the streets of the Windy City with a long-bladed hunting knife until he found a 19-year-old prostitute. He stabbed her 30 times.

TURNER: Passion

Nightmare on Leicester Square

A BOY of 17 made a lethal claw out of a glove and surgical blades . . . after watching a hideous horror film about a psychopathic child killer, a court heard on Tuesday.

Chester James of Hoiland Walk, Upper Holloway, was "inspired" by the smash-hit "Nightmare on Elm Street" - which he should not even have seen at his age.

In the movie a disfigured monster calles Freddie Kreuger wears a glove with long knives fixed in the fingers to slice up kids.

A poster for the film shows him wearing the bladed glove.

Snarebrook Crown Court was told that James had a home-made replica when he was arrested on his way to a party.

He had used a thick gardening glove, reinforced the fingers with cardboard and stuck five surgical blades on the ends with tape.

Outrage over boy's horror movie weapon

Police made an unusual request for the glove not to be destroyed - so it could be displayed at Scotland Yard's Black Museum alongside Britain's most horrendous weapons.

The judge, Mr Recorder Nicholas Miscampbell said:

"It's the most horrific offensive weapon I have ever seen in my life. It could disfigure someone in the extreme."

James's barrister, Monroe Carr said: "One may wonder how a young boy would have the imagination to make such a hideous thing?

"The inspiration came from a film that can be watched at the cinema called "Nightmare on Elm Street" which features a glove like this.

"Had the defendent not seen this film he could not have made such an horrific weapon."

The court heard that some of the boy's teenage friends had also made the glove and the youngsters compared them to see which was the best.

James admitted carrying an offensive weapon in Leicester Square in August last year and was put on probation for two years.

© *Video Trade Weekly,*
8 April 1991

MAIL ATTACKS ABBOTT

BVA response fails to prevent counterblast

EIGHT years after its "video nasties" campaign, the *Daily Mail* has renewed its feud with video by attacking British Videogram Association director-general Norman Abbott.

A long article by columnist Lynda Lee-Potter last Tuesday (April 3), under the headline "Ban This Porn Before It Destroys Our Children", claimed statements by Abbott were "moronic" and "smug".

The article is the second by Lee-Potter in recent weeks attacking the video industry,

claiming it makes violent films available to children.

Abbott replied to the first article in a letter which was printed in the 1.7 million circulation *Mail*. Lee-Potter has seized on his comments as the basis for her latest piece. His letter is blasted as "moronic".

The latest article says people wrote in their "overwhelming hundreds" after the last piece to say that sick videos are an "incitement to violent sexual crime" and that those who watch them develop an appetite for "bestial torture which becomes insatiable".

Lee-Potter criticises Abbott for saying banning certain titles would create a black market. She wrote that the letters she has received telling of children watching videos "make nonsense of Norman Abbott's smug statement that 'Anyone who sells or rents a video to an underage customer is breaking the law'".

Abbott said that the BVA was discussing how to respond to the

The article which attacked BVA chief, Norman Abbott (top).

article and was likely to ask for a meeting with the *Mail* editor or Lee-Potter herself.

He added: "This is just a sensationalist type of argument. The whole thing is pathetic."

He said the article was confusing and did not explain what Lee-Potter was calling for – did

she want the banning of 18-rated films, more enforcement of the existing law or stricter punishments for lawbreakers?

In the same issue, the *Mail* carried an ad for the generic campaign.

■   **See Editorial, page 32.**

BAN THIS PORN BEFORE IT DESTROYS OUR CHILDREN!

(article by Lynda Lee-Potter, *Daily Mail*, 3/4/91)

I recently asked you to tell me what you thought about the dangerous effects of increasingly obscene videos which can be rented in every city, small town and village.

'Cynical entrepreneurs who produce this sickening material are becoming richer and bolder', I wrote. 'They are prepared to go to any lengths to satisfy the market, to fulfil the basest instincts in human nature'.

You replied in your overwhelming hundreds confirming my own belief that sick videos are a terrifying incitement to violent sexual crime, that those who watch them develop an appetite for bestial torture which becomes insatiable.

In the future I believe we will look back in horror and incredulity at material which was allowed to be legally on sale. 'The law has no teeth', I added, and predictably there was a moronic letter from the Director General of the British Videogram Association, Norman Abbott, saying that banning certain videos would only create a lucrative black market.

This is as daft as protesting that if we made crime legal it would be cheaper because we wouldn't need jails or policemen.

So many of you told of discovering with horror that your own children had watched obscene videos at the homes of friends. Some mothers only learnt what had happened when their child woke screaming in terror in the night.

Mary Land writes from Lechdale: 'My friends who have children at the local primary school say that some of the pupils openly talk of the sex scenes they have seen on videos hired by their parents'.

This certainly makes nonsense of Norman Abbott's smug statement that 'Anyone who sells or rents a video to an under-age customer is breaking the law'. And is it surprising that seven-year-olds have been found playing 'Rapists' in the school playgrounds?

There are also sad and disturbing letters from the wives of professional men who have become so hooked on these videos it is destroying previously happy marriages.

'What makes matters worse', says one wife who does not want to be named, 'is the fact that my husband invites other men to the house to watch and to exchange films.

'They are contacts he makes through a sordid magazine. The people with whom my husband comes into contact with in his everyday life would never suspect he had become interested in this kind of behaviour'.

These women clearly feel a personal sense of shame and their letters are heartbreaking to read. They certainly confirm the fact that those who become addicted want to watch increasingly nasty material. Other readers mention their fears that children who see videos of torture and bestiality won't be able to differentiate between reality and fantasy.

Brian Hunt writes from Burnham on Crouch: 'Even where a child realises he has watched fiction, the appalling images are going to be ever-present in his mind. We know from damaged children how childhood experiences often re-emerge in adults making them social, mental and emotional cripples unable to lead normal lives'.

I had many letters from men and women still suffering nightmares from films they saw 20 or more years ago and which would seem innocuous today. Sadly almost nobody has any confidence in the commitment or desire of politicians to do anything constructive. Again and again people made passionate pleas to the *Daily Mail*.

Doreen Barker of Ledbury, Herefordshire, writes: 'I have faith in the ability of your newspaper to pursue another of its relentless, vigorous campaigns to the bitter end to have this terrible business stopped'.

And it is a terrible business, a subterranean pit of evil that is becoming deeper, more enveloping, more horrible. I repeat that the law has no teeth and the battered old molars it does have are not being effectively applied.

The law must be strengthened and clarified. Our main aim must be to empty the shelves of our videos shops of sick and disgusting films which are readily and cheaply for hire.

It's a campaign in which every parent teacher association, every young wives group, every political party in every small town ought to participate. In the knowledge that we are battling for the future sanity of our children.

Video contents

Interviews

| Clip 1 | *Going Live!* | 5 min. 51 sec. |
| Clip 2 | *Film '92* | 7 min. 30 sec. |

Textual Analysis

| Clip 3 | *The Wild One* | 'PG' 9 min. 30 sec. |

Nudity

Clip 4	*Sheena, Queen of the Jungle*	'15' 2 min. 5 sec.
Clip 5	*The Delinquents*	'12' 1 min. 47 sec.
Clip 6	*A Room With a View*	'PG' 3 min.

Film synopses

Sheena - Queen of the Jungle
John Quillerman, 1984. 'Female Tarzan stuff about a girl raised by an African tribe when her explorer parents are killed. She goes on to wear a suede bikini and fall for a visiting journalist.' (*Guardian* preview screened 3.15 a.m. Friday 31 December 1993.)

The Delinquents
Chris Thomson, 1989. Two teenagers ignore adult disapproval and fall in love. Kylie Minogue stars.

A Room With a View
James Ivory, 1985. 'Upper-class mores are put under the microscope in of one those typically British class-conscious studies. The story is of a young couple who indulge in a passionate affair while on holiday in Florence. A detailed period tale adapted by Ruth Prawer Jhabvala from the novel by E. M. Forster.' *(Elliot's Guide to Films on Video, 1990.)*

Addresses and sources

The following institutions specialise in areas that relate to Media Education and can offer support of various kinds to teachers. (Do not encourage students to write to them.)

British Board of Film (and Video) Classification (BBFC)
3 Soho Square
London W1V 5DE

Advertising Standards Authority (ASA Ltd)
Brook House
2-16 Torrington Place
London WC1E 7HN

British Film Institute
Teaching materials and books relating to media and media education.
BFI Publications
29 Rathbone Street
London W1P 1AG

BFI Education
INSET and other events, advice.
21 Stephen Street
London W1P 1PL

Arts Council of Great Britain
Publications and funding.
14 Great Peter Street
London SW1P 3NG

English and Media Centre, London
Publish range of books, classroom materials for English and Media teachers. Order from:
National Association for the Teaching of English (NATE)
Birley School Annexe
Fox Lane Site
Frecheville
Fox Lane
Sheffield S12 4WY

Film Education
Publications, visits and events.
5th Floor
41-42 Berners Street
London W1P 3AA

Media Education Centre
INSET, publications and events.
5 Llandaff Road
Canton
Cardiff CF1 9NF

MOMI Education
Teaching materials and presentations relating to the Museum; INSET, events for schools.
Museum of the Moving Image
South Bank
London SE1 8XT

National Museum of Photography, Film and Television
Teaching materials and presentations relating to the Museum; INSET, events for schools.
Princes View
Bradford
West Yorkshire BD7 0TR

Newspaper Society
Publications, teaching materials, INSET, annual Newspapers in Education Week each October.
74-77 Great Russell Street
London WC1B 1NR

Northern Ireland Film Council
Recently established: aims to provide publications, advice, events and INSET.
7 Lower Crescent
Belfast BT7 1NR

Scottish Film Council
INSET, publications, events, research.
Dowanhill
74 Victoria Crescent Road
Glasgow G11 9JN

Also available from BFI Publishing

HANDS ON

A Teacher's Guide to Media Technology

Roy Stafford

The first comprehensive introductory guide to the burgeoning range of media technologies now available to teachers. Each of the four main chapters (on video, audio, photography and computers) offers a discussion of the appropriate equipment, a detailed presentation of basic techniques and suggestions for classroom activity. A substantial reference system looks at the development of media education, the current state of curriculum development, information on equipment and support organisations. Includes bibliography and glossary.

'The book successfully shows that practical work is not an add-on extra in media education ... If one agrees that the more you know, the better off you are, then *Hands On* should become an indispensable part of any media teacher's resources.' *In the Picture*

ISBN 0 85170 385 2
Pb £19.95

SCREENING MIDDLEMARCH

19th Century Novel to 90s Television

Edited by Cary Bazalgette and Christine James

A unique resource for Media Studies and A-Level English teachers and students. Its multimedia approach - closely linking with the BBC dramatisation - encourages an understanding of the creative, logistical and budgetary processes involved in a major international co-production. The pack looks at key concepts such as Narrative, Realism and Institution. Contains workbook, video and audio tape.

ISBN 1 87423 937 1
Pack £67.25

LIGHTS, CAMERA, ACTION!

Careers in Film, Television and Video

Josephine Langham

Film and television seem to offer the kind of interesting and well-paid jobs that young people want. But in the past few years the media industries have undergone massive change. For only £9.95 this accessible and comprehensive handbook provides up-to-date information about opportunities available within the fields of film, television and video.

'A no-nonsense guide to the businesses of film, TV and video.' *Empire*

ISBN 0 85170 343 7
Pb £9.95

Lights, Camera, Action! offers sound advice on:

- **types of jobs available**

- **educational qualifications required**

- **training provision**

- **the NVQ system**

- **new technical developments affecting employment**

- **the first steps along a career path**

MEDIA COURSES UK

Edited by Lavinia Orton

Media Courses UK gives practical and up-to-date information on media courses available throughout the United Kingdom. This includes: topics covered in the syllabus, qualifications needed for entry, course length, proportions of practical and academic work, kinds of qualifications on offer, plus courses combining media with other subjects. An annual publication.

ISBN 0 85170 498 0
Pb £7.95

BFI books are available from all good bookshops or by mail from:
BFI Publications, 29-35 Rathbone Street, London, W1P 1AG
Credit card orders, telephone: 071 636 3289
Please add £1.00 per book for post and packing and allow 28 days for delivery